W9-BZM-883

The Eberly Library
Waynesburg College
Waynesburg, Pennsylvania

MR MOODY AND THE EVANGELICAL TRADITION

MR MOODY AND THE EVANGELICAL TRADITION

Edited by
TIMOTHY GEORGE

T & T CLARK INTERNATIONAL
A Continuum imprint
LONDON • NEW YORK

T&T CLARK INTERNATIONAL LTD

A Continuum imprint

The Tower Building   15 East 26th St.
11 York Road   New York
London SE1 7NX, UK   NY 10010, USA

www.tandtclark.com

British Library Cataloguing-in-Publication Data
A catalogue record for this book is available from the British Library.

ISBN 0 567 08494 9 (Hardback)

Typeset by RefineCatch Limited, Bungay, Suffolk
Printed and bound in Great Britain by MPG Books Ltd, Bodmin, Cornwall

For
Thomas E. Corts
Marla Haas Corts

Their devotion to the flame of Drummond
and Moody has helped pass on the
torch to the rising generation

CONTENTS

CONTRIBUTORS

Professor D. W. BEBBINGTON
Department of History, University of Stirling, Scotland

The Reverend Dr RICHARD THOMAS BEWES
Rector of All Souls, Langham Place, London, England

Dr THOMAS E. CORTS
President, Samford University, Birmingham, Alabama
United States of America

Dr LYLE W. DORSETT
Professor of Christian Ministries and Evangelism
Wheaton College, Wheaton, Illinois
United States of America

The late Professor LEWIS A. DRUMMOND
Former Chancellor of School of Evangelism
Billy Graham Evangelical Association,
Asheville, North Carolina
United States of America

The Reverend Dr TIMOTHY GEORGE
Dean, Beeson Divinity School, Samford University,
Birmingham, Alabama
United States of America

Dr STANLEY N. GUNDRY
Vice President and Editor-in-Chief, Zondervan Publishing
House, Grand Rapids, Michigan
United States of America

Professor DONALD P. HUSTAD
Senior Professor of Church Music and Worship
Southern Baptist Theological Seminary, Louisville, Kentucky
United States of America

MR MOODY AND THE EVANGELICAL TRADITION

The Reverend DON SWEETING
Pastor, Cherry Creek Presbyterian Church, Denver, Colorado
United States of America

The Reverend Dr DEREK TIDBALL
Principal, London Bible College
London, England

The Reverend Dr WARREN W. WIERSBE
Former Pastor, Moody Church, Chicago, Illinois
United States of America

INTRODUCTION:
REMEMBERING MR MOODY

Timothy George

On 22 December 1899, Dwight Lyman Moody died in North-field, Massachusetts, the same small New England town in which he had been born twenty-four years before the American Civil War began. Newspapers around the world echoed the headlines of the *New York Times*: 'Dwight L. Moody is dead.' Years before, Moody had anticipated this moment in a famous quip: 'Someday you will read in the papers that D. L. Moody of East Northfield is dead. Don't you believe a word of it! At that moment I shall be more alive than I am now. I shall have gone up higher, that is all . . . I was born of the flesh in 1837. I was born of the Spirit in 1856. That which is born of the flesh may die. That which is born of the spirit will live forever.'

More than a century later, Moody's influence and his legacy continue to shape the evangelical world in many ways. Moody has been called the Billy Graham of the nineteenth century, but it would be more accurate to say that Graham became the D. L. Moody of the twentieth. Both are evangelical icons in the revivalist tradition of Jonathan Edwards, George Whitefield, Charles G. Finney and Billy Sunday. Both were admired and listened to by American presidents; Moody preached to Abraham Lincoln and U. S. Grant. Both were best-selling authors and institution-shapers as well as fervent gospel preachers who moved the masses by their campaigns and crusades. And, like Graham, Moody avoided the taint of scandal in both personal and financial matters, modelling the virtues of integrity, sincerity and single-mindedness. In their respective eras, both men also served as magnanimous leaders around whom others could rally. While Graham's global outreach and world-historical impact has exceeded that of Moody, it is no insult to say that without D. L. Moody, there would have been no Billy Graham. Without meaning to do so really, Moody was the founder of contemporary interdenominational evangelicalism.

Moody's background gave few hints of his future greatness. He was the sixth of nine children born to Edwin, a skilled mason, and his wife Betsey. He was only four when his father died and his mother joined the local Unitarian church. The minister was a moderate which probably explains why he baptized the Moody children in the name of the Triune God. Later Betsey Moody embraced a more orthodox faith under the preaching of her famous son. Though Moody would later become a great apostle to the cities, he never escaped his small-town culture and lack of formal training. Never educated beyond the fifth grade, his spelling was atrocious and his pronunciation quaint. C. H. Spurgeon once remarked that Moody was the only man who could say 'Mesopotamia' in two syllables! At age seventeen, Moody set out for Boston where he found a job selling shoes in a store run by his uncle. Seeking his bearings, he joined a local Sunday School class whose teacher, Edward Kimball, took a special interest in Moody, leading him to trust in Christ and guiding him into membership in the Congregational church. Today a plaque on Boston's Court Street marks the site of his conversion, an event little noted at the time. Although Moody had received little religious instruction at this point, those who knew him were impressed by his 'earnest determination to be a Christian'.

Leaving his native New England for Chicago in 1856, Moody came under the influence of the lay-led prayer revival which swept through the urban centres of America on the eve of the Civil War. Just as Kimball had encouraged his first decisive steps in Christian faith in Boston, so too in Chicago he was discipled by 'Mother' Phillips, a formidable woman of faith who taught him to study the Bible and to reach out in love to the unwanted street children of Chicago. Moody started his own Sunday School which eventually attracted more than one thousand students. From this work would emerge the Illinois Street congregation which later evolved into the Moody Memorial Church. Not everyone approved of Moody's work with these castaways and ragamuffins. He was dubbed 'Crazy Moody' and criticized for enticing the children to Sunday School with the promise of pony rides and special gifts, his 'missionary sugar'. Others objected to the fact that a mere layman, uneducated and not ordained, should usurp the role of better trained clergy.

But Moody's great compassion for the children, and his obvious success in this ministry, could not be gainsaid. All the while Moody was rising through the ranks of the Chicago mercantile world, becoming a very successful salesman. Through his work with the YMCA, Moody met a number of Chicago's business leaders, including John Farwell and Cyrus McCormick, who became key financial backers of his evangelistic endeavours. From serving on the YMCA Committee to Visit Sick Members and Strangers, Moody rose to the office of President. At this time the YMCA had an explicitly evangelical agenda requiring its members, for example, to embrace 'justification by faith in Christ alone'. This meshed well with Moody's own concerns and his work with the Association became a platform for a wider ministry.

Moody's life during the turbulent decade of the 1860s appears to be a frenetic blur of activity. Moody later said, 'I never knew a lazy man to become a Christian. I have known gamblers and drunkards and saloon-keepers to be converted, but never a lazy man.' During these years Moody himself was far from idle: he married Emma Revell, a fellow Sunday School worker who provided whatever polish he was to have in later life; he served as a chaplain for the Union cause in the Civil War making several trips to the front; he intensified his work as a city missionary in Chicago; he oversaw the construction of new buildings; he made his first trip to Great Britain where he gave many sermons and lectures. He once noted that the New Testament does not speak of the resolutions of the Apostles but of the Acts!

Moody's intense activism was matched by a keen sense of urgency. In 1867, a newspaper reporter visited Moody's Chicago congregation and wrote down his impression:

When Moody speaks, everybody listens. Even those who do not like him. His remarks are short, pithy and practical, and his exhortations impressive and sometimes touching even to tears. . . . His remarks always have a martial ring. He wants 'to wrest this State from the power of Satan and take and hold it for Christ'. What he wants Done he wants Done Now. . . . As a brother once said of him, 'he acts as if he were going to convert the world off-hand'.

Little wonder, then, that even the irrepressible Moody felt exhausted and nearly burnt out.

In 1871, two events conspired to redirect his ministry. The great Chicago fire left him homeless and open to new opportunities to preach the Gospel abroad. This was also a time of great spiritual agony for Moody that came to a climax in New York City in an unforgettable experience of surrender and supernatural empowerment. Moody himself described the transformation: 'I was all the time tugging and carrying water. But now I have a river that carries me.' From this moment on, his friend D. W. Whittle said, 'Moody lost interest in everything except the preaching of Christ and working for souls'. Moody was reticent to use his own dramatic experience as a benchmark for others, but he increasingly stressed the importance of the Spirit's anointing for Christian growth and service.

Moody's enduring legacy as the most successful transatlantic evangelist of his time was secured by his phenomenal two-year campaign (1873–5) in the major cities of Ireland, Scotland and England. Moody and his musical associate, Ira D. Sankey, criss-crossed the British Isles, attracting millions of people to their meetings, from ruffians to royalty. The evangelist's return to North America brought similar results. Soon, 'Mr Moody' became a household name.

Moody's success as an evangelist must be set in the context of the Gilded Age, an era of urbanization and rapid industrial growth. Moody has been criticized for preaching an individualistic gospel while ignoring deeper, systemic evils. Yet Moody did criticize employers for 'sweating' their workers and for paying them starvation wages. He was also an ardent abolitionist and challenged racial discrimination in the Reconstructionist South. As an evangelist, Moody travelled more than a million miles and addressed more than one hundred million people, all in an age without aeroplanes or microphones. Moody's meetings were marked by careful planning and savvy marketing, but he respected the sovereignty of the Holy Spirit in salvation and the integrity of each individual's spiritual struggle.

Moody was a vigorous, muscular Christian who, according to one English observer, had a 'terrier-like aspect'. The rapid pace and excitement of his messages led to a concluding crescendo that 'was like a cavalry charge. You had either to go with it or get out of the way.' Yet Moody held this kind of bravura in perfect equipoise with the most heartfelt tenderness. Sankey's sentimental songs were matched note for note by Moody's stories and anecdotes. One can hear echoes of the kind of narrative power that arrested so many in this sample of the evangelist's preaching:

> I can imagine when Christ said to the little band around Him, 'Go ye into all the world and preach the gospel,' Peter said, 'Lord, do you really mean that we are to go back to Jerusalem and preach the gospel to those men that murdered you?' 'Yes,' said Christ, 'go, hunt up that man that spat in my face, tell him he may have a seat in my kingdom yet. Yes, Peter, go find that man that made that cruel crown of thorns and placed it on my brow, and tell him I will have a crown ready for him when he comes into my kingdom, and there will be no thorns in it. Hunt up that man that took a reed and brought it down over the cruel thorns, driving them into my brow, and tell him I will put a scepter in his hand, and he shall rule over the nations of the earth, if he will accept salvation. Search for the man that drove the spear into my side, and tell him there is a nearer way to my heart than that. Tell him I forgive him freely, and that he can be saved if he will accept salvation as a gift.'

Contrary to popular opinion, Moody's preaching was theologically driven, structured around what the evangelist called the 'Three R*s*' of the Bible: *ruined* by the Fall, *redeemed* by the Blood and *regenerated* by the Spirit. If Moody preached more about the love of God than the torments of hell, he did not deny the latter. Moody believed in the inerrancy and verbal inspiration of the Bible – 'We ought to open the Holy Book as we would go into a sanctuary where we were sure of meeting our heavenly Father face to face, of hearing His voice' – though he counted among his close friends liberal evangelicals with less strict views of inspiration.

No doubt, Moody's lack of formal theological training left him vulnerable to the attacks of unbelieving critics. Revivalism in general, and Moody in particular, have been accused of contributing to the evacuation of the evangelical mind, and there is some truth to this. Evangelistic goodwill and warm-hearted piety alone were not enough to stave off the inroads of liberalism and unbelieving theology in the decades after

Moody's death. Yet Moody was deeply grieved by the divisions he witnessed within the Christian family, and he longed for the day, he said, when all bickering, division and party feeling would cease, when even Roman Catholics and Protestants would see eye to eye and march together in a solid column against the forces of the Evil One.

Indeed, Moody's openness to Catholics was remarkable for the times. In Northfield, he contributed funds for building a local Catholic church despite the 'muttering of the rabid antipapists', as his son Paul characterized the reaction of certain staunch Protestants. He also welcomed Catholic leaders to the platform of his 1893 Chicago campaign. Despite these initiatives of goodwill, though, Moody did not advocate an uncritical ecumenism. While preaching in Dublin, Ireland, he challenged the Catholic doctrine of purgatory and spoke against priestly confessions. He also broke with his sometime associate, the temperance leader Frances Willard, because of her association with Unitarians who denied the divinity of Christ. Moody's overriding concern was that the gospel of Jesus Christ be proclaimed to all people everywhere. For this reason, he opposed what he called 'this miserable sectarian spirit' among orthodox believers.

The essays in this volume present a mosaic of Moody's life and legacy, reflecting several facets of his work as an evangelist, preacher, social reformer, publisher, founder of schools and inter-national evangelical celebrity. In 1999, the centenary of Moody's death, Beeson Divinity School of Samford University, in cooperation with London Bible College and the University of Edinburgh's New College, sponsored a series of symposia celebrating Moody's contributions to the evangelical tradition and examining his enduring influence on recent religious trends. The essays gathered here were originally presented at one or more of these symposia.

The symposium at London Bible College was marked by the presence of the Reverend Dr John Pollock, whose notable biography of Moody was first published in 1963. Looking back on his Moody research, Pollock commented:

> When I began to delve into D. L. Moody's original letters in the archives at Chicago and at Northfield, Massachusetts, I had little knowledge of his story or character beyond an awareness of a massive and unusual American who crossed and re-crossed the

story of British religion in the nineteenth century and strongly marked his own country. As I read through letter after letter in his unpunctuated, misspelt scrawl, and waded through the great bulk of printed material, I could not fail to be impressed by the astonishing events of his swift rise to fame and power: in 1873 he landed at Liverpool utterly obscure, in 1875 he sailed away with Scotland, Ireland and England at his feet. And the more I read, the more I enjoyed this warm-hearted, strong-willed, genial heavyweight.

This occasion also marked the announcement of the John Pollock Award for Christian Biography, an annual competition sponsored by Beeson Divinity School for outstanding biographical writing. Each year publishers and readers alike nominate recent biographies of quality about Christian leaders past or present for consideration in this competition.

While London had been the scene of Moody's largest revival gatherings in the British Isles, he had first risen to fame in the great campaigns of 1873 in Edinburgh and Glasgow. The Edinburgh Moody symposium took place at New College's Martin Hall where some 100 historians, theologians, students and church leaders gathered to discuss the historic impact of Moody's ministry. Speakers at this festive commemoration included President Thomas E. Corts of Samford University and Professor David W. Bebbington of the University of Stirling. Among those participating in the discussion were Professor Thomas F. Torrance and Professor James B. Torrance. Two years earlier, in 1997, Beeson Divinity School had collaborated with New College and the University of St Andrews in sponsoring a centennial celebration of the legacy of Henry Drummond, the Scottish college evangelist who became one of Moody's closest friends and staunchest supporters. Although Drummond was fourteen years younger than Moody, his untimely death took place two years before that of his American friend. At Drummond's death in 1897, Moody said: 'Never have I known a man who, in my opinion, lived nearer the Master, or sought to do his will more fully.' The papers from the Edinburgh Drummond symposium have been edited by Thomas E. Corts and published as *Henry Drummond: A Perpetual Benediction* (T & T Clark, 1999).

Drawing on the London and Edinburgh Moody celebrations,

an American commemoration of Moody's work took place on 28 September 1999 at Beeson Divinity School on the campus of Samford University, under the rubric, 'Love Them In: A Centennial Celebration of the Life and Legacy of D. L. Moody, 1899–1999'. In addition to the scholarly presentations at this symposium, the American festivities also included a service of worship held in Beeson's Andrew Gerow Hodges Chapel. The musical contribution of Ira D. Sankey was acknowledged in a hymn festival of his famous gospel songs, and a sermon presented by The Reverend Dr Warren W. Wiersbe. This service also featured a rare recording of Moody reading the Beatitudes and Sankey singing 'God Be With You Till We Meet Again'. These items were provided by the Moody Bible Institute archives.

Stanley N. Gundry's essay, 'Demythologizing Moody', introduces us to conflicting interpretations about Moody and the various 'myths' about his theological views propagated over the past century by friend and foe alike. Although Moody was not a professional theologian, he was possessed of deep doctrinal convictions and stayed within the framework of evangelical Protestant orthodoxy. Gundry refutes the charges of later interpreters who portrayed Moody as the fountainhead of pentecostalism, perfectionism and dispensationalism. While Moody did not oppose these emerging evangelical belief systems, his overriding concern was to reach out to the masses with the simple gospel of Jesus Christ. Likewise, during the Fundamentalist–Modernist Controversy of the 1920s, both sides tried to claim Moody's mantle for themselves, but, as Gundry shows, this kind of attempt to bowdlerize history leads nowhere. A more interesting, though still hypothetical, question would be: Had Moody lived another two decades, would the evangelical movement have fallen into such polarized competing camps?

Lyle Dorsett's impressive biography of Moody bears the title, *A Passion for Souls* (Moody Press, 1997). However, in his essay, 'D. L. Moody: More than an Evangelist', Dorsett shows that Moody's calling to work with souls encompassed healing and nurture as well as evangelistic rescue in the narrow sense. Dorsett traces Moody's social outreach and philanthropic concerns to his early ministry among the street urchins of Chicago and to his service as a chaplain to soldiers on the battlefields of the Civil War. Moody persistently refused to divorce conversion from discipleship. He would have agreed with the statement of the great Methodist missionary to India, E. Stanley Jones: A soul without a body is a ghost; a body without a soul is a corpse. The gospel is addressed to living persons, soul and body, in all of their broken humanity and need for wholeness.

In 'The Great Turning Point in the Life of D. L. Moody', Don Sweeting looks at the impact of the great Chicago fire of 1871 on Moody's life and work. Having lost his home, church and nearly everything in this great disaster, Moody unexpectedly found new directions and a much wider scope for his future witness. The images are compelling: Moody's family fleeing the fire in a horse and buggy; Sankey sitting alone in a rowing boat on Lake Michigan while Chicago burned. But, as Sweeting shows, this traumatic event was the catalyst for Moody's spiritual breakthrough and the transformation of his ministry that followed.

The essay by Thomas E. Corts, 'D. L. Moody: Payment on Account', reviews the remarkable, and still somewhat inexplicable, impact of Moody and Sankey, a shoe salesman and a bank clerk, on the religious life of Great Britain. The numbers alone are astounding. On one occasion, Moody preached to an overflow crowd of 40,000 people who could not find seats inside the great Crystal Palace in Glasgow for his final meeting there. During his 1875 campaign in London, which stretched from March to July, Moody held 80–85 meetings and spoke to 2.5 million people. But numbers alone do not tell the whole story, and Corts traces the extent of Moody's outreach to many persons of diverse races, classes, genders and denominations, his appeal to university students and aristocratic élites as well as to the masses of common folk who thronged to hear him. Also in view here are the deep and transforming friendships Moody enjoyed with many leading figures in Victorian Britain, from the saintly William Pennefather, the evangelical Anglican leader who invited Moody to England in 1873, to Charles Haddon Spurgeon, London's famous Baptist icon who opened the pulpit of his Metropolitan Tabernacle to Moody. As Corts points out, despite Moody's enormous fame, he did not succumb to the blandishments of popular success but retained an integrity and humility that impressed even his critics.

D. W. Bebbington is a Scottish Baptist historian who participated in both the Moody and Drummond symposia in Edinburgh. In his essay on 'D. L. Moody as a Transatlantic Evangelical', Bebbington traces Moody's revivalist success against the background of criticism from his detractors. Bebbington also presents Moody as one of the formative shapers of the transatlantic evangelical coalition: Moody's six trips to Great Britain also had great impact on American religion as many of Moody's British friends became popular speakers at the famous Northfield conferences. Bebbington has offered one of the most convincing typologies of modern evangelicalism as a movement centred on conversion, the Bible, the cross and activism. In each of these ways, he says, Moody was an archetypal evangelical.

Drawing on and qualifying Iain Murray's distinction between 'revival' and 'revivalism', the late Lewis A. Drummond portrays Moody as an exemplar of both. While Moody, like Charles G. Finney before him, was a great organizer and innovator in revivalist methodology, he was neither exploitive nor insensitive in his efforts to reach as many souls as possible with a message of Christ. While allowing that revival is best understood as a Spirit-directed 'surprising work of God', as Jonathan Edwards described the Awakening in his day, Drummond nonetheless sees an important role for revivalists like Moody who are used to bring many persons into the life of faith during seasons when 'true revivals' are few and far between.

Donald P. Hustad, an outstanding musician and sometime organist for the Billy Graham Evangelistic Association, explores the theme of 'D. L. Moody and Church Music'. He examines the legacy of Ira D. Sankey, Moody's song leader and sidekick, who 'sang the Gospel' as faithfully as Moody preached it. The Moody-Sankey gospel hymnbooks became bestsellers and provided enormous income for Moody's educational and philanthropic enterprises. Hustad points to Sankey's continuing influence on hymnody and contemporary church music in the evangelical tradition.

Derek Tidball, principal of the London Bible College, presents an analysis of a single Moody sermon, one which took as its theme the supernatural power of the Holy Spirit 'in' and 'upon' the yielded believer. The theme of this sermon became one of the most persistent notes in Moody's preaching. Moody was fond of saying that 'you cannot improve the water supply by painting the pump'. Moody knew by experience that activism alone, without the inner renewal of the Spirit, would lead to barrenness and exhaustion. Without such spiritual anointing, Moody felt, all of his entrepreneurial abilities would have been in vain. This chapter also reveals Moody as a preacher who spoke to the heart in a simple and compelling manner, without rhetorical embellishment or theological hair-splitting.

Warren W. Wiersbe himself stands in the best tradition of Moody as an effective communicator of the Gospel to the masses. As a former senior pastor of the Moody Memorial Church in Chicago, and as the general director of the well-known Back to the Bible Broadcast, Wiersbe has had a distinguished ministry of preaching and teaching the Scriptures, and he has done so with the kind of urgency that motivated Moody as well. In the sermon included here, Wiersbe reflects on Moody's favourite Bible text, 1 John 2:17, 'He that doeth the will of God abideth forever.' This verse was framed and hung in Moody's office, and still stands as an epitaph on his grave at Northfield.

Richard Thomas Bewes, rector of All Souls Church, Langham Place, London, tells the moving story of how his own grandfather, Tommy Bewes, was taken as a young lad to a Moody campaign in Plymouth, England on 26 September 1882. In 'One Sermon was Enough: A Family's Testimony', Bewes discloses how the transformation that took place in little Tommy Bewes that evening has issued in a remarkable family history of devotion to Christ and Christian service. This brief but moving account is a fitting conclusion to this volume for it reveals the enormous influence that can flow from one single life touched and changed for ever by the Gospel of Jesus Christ.

As an appendix to this volume, we have included a contemporary account and reflection on Moody by his devoted friend, Henry Drummond. Drummond is best remembered as the man who wrote *The Greatest Thing in the World*, a devotional commentary on 1 Corinthians 13, first given as an extemporaneous talk to Christian workers in England when Drummond was persuaded to 'fill in' for Moody at the latter's request. Drummond was a scholar and scientist with a strong interest in an evolutionary model of relating science and religion in the wake of Darwin's writings. But Drummond's interest in evolution was combined with a strong evangelical piety and deep devotion to the person of Jesus Christ. In an exchange with Ira D. Sankey near the end of his life, Drummond reaffirmed his long-held beliefs in the cross of Christ, the forgiveness of sins, the hope of immortality based on Christ's resurrection and the necessity of personal conversion.[1] Moody was criticized for inviting Drummond to speak at his Northfield conference, but he defended Drummond with these words: 'I've been shown that he is a better man than I am, and, therefore he should speak.' Moody and Drummond were possessed of a fierce loyalty to one another. In the biographical sketch presented here, Drummond does his best to present 'just the right impression of Mr Moody' against some of the caricatures and misunderstandings that prevailed at the time. Drummond's account of Moody's life and work, 'Mr. Moody: Some Impressions and Facts', was originally published in the December 1894 issue of *McClure's Magazine* (volume 4, no. 1).

During Moody's life, it was said that 'the world has yet to see what God will do, with, and for, and through, and in, and by, the man who is fully and holy consecrated to him'. Moody, by God's grace, sought to be such a person. And by God's grace, he was.

I

DEMYTHOLOGIZING MOODY

Stanley N. Gundry

INTRODUCTION

At Moody's funeral Theodore Cuyler estimated that at times Moody spoke to 40,000–50,000 people a week, an estimate not at all unreasonable in view of the fact that often 10,000–20,000 people were in the audience. When Moody preached, the local newspapers would carry a full account of the previous day's meeting, often with a verbatim stenographer's report of Moody's message – all of this on the front page, not buried in the religion section. In this light, A. T. Pierson's estimate that he brought the claims of Christ to 100 million people may err on the conservative side. This is all the more remarkable when we remember that he did all this without most of the modern technology that we have come to take for granted – public address systems, radio, television, satellite uplinks, jet travel and now even the Internet.

An admiring biographer, Charles R. Erdman, said that at the close of his life Moody was the 'most famous and influential evangelist in the world'.[1] More recently a less sympathetic historian, Ernest Sandeen, spoke of Moody as 'the most influential "clergyman" in America' in the last two decades of the nineteenth century. And none other than Martin Marty has written that at a critical stage of American religious history Moody 'could plausibly have been called Mr Revivalist and perhaps even Mr Protestant'.[2] But this man who insisted he simply be called 'Mr Moody' had no formal theological education, had the very dubious equivalent of only a fourth- or fifth-grade education, and was never ordained to the ministry.

After they pass from the scene, individuals of such accomplishment fall victim to both friend and foe. The eulogistic biographers tend to touch up their portraits to eliminate the warts and blemishes. Another class of historians, the 'debunkers', does its level best to discredit its subjects and to portray them as anything but what they claimed or appeared to be. The institutions founded or shaped by these individuals want to be viewed as their legitimate successors, but in supporting those claims they often ignore certain uncomfortable facts about their founders, or worse yet they engage in revisionist history. And as for the rest of us – well, it is only natural that we would like to have our heroes support those beliefs and practices that we hold dear.

However, with an individual like Moody it is important to know him as he really was, for only then can we truly know him for what made him great, and only then can we learn from his weaknesses and mistakes.

Over the years a multifaceted mythology has developed around Dwight L. Moody. We can summarize the main features of the Moody myth in the following statements: 1. In Moody method triumphed over message; 2. Moody's revivalist/ evangelistic methodology was in logical and historical succession from Charles Finney; 3. Moody was a Pentecostal before Pentecostalism; 4. Moody was a perfectionist and espoused second blessing theology; 5. Moody was a dispensationalist; 6. Moody rejected the substitutionary view of the atonement in favour of the moral influence theory of the atonement; 7. Moody was either an incipient theological liberal or a fundamentalist.[3]

The myths/the realities

In Moody method triumphed over message
This claim takes a variety of forms and most frequently comes from historians who have no particular sympathy with Moody, from critics who feel that in Moody legitimate theological concerns were shortchanged, or from admirers who like the alleged fact that Moody sat very loose to theological issues.

Now before we go any further, it is important to acknowledge one thing. By no stretch of the imagination was Moody a trained theologian; nor did he tend to think systematically about such issues. But at the same time, all of us are theologians, whether or not we like it or acknowledge it. Moody is no exception. So the task with Moody is to go to his sermons to discover his implicit and explicit attitudes toward theology in general and doctrine in particular.

In a 1973 thesis by Stan Nussbaum we find one of the more severe criticisms that, for Moody, 'theology, as least as a systematic discipline, is superfluous to Christian faith'.

1. Theology is basically superfluous to salvation and therefore wastes precious time.

2. Theology will not stand against the devil because it is based on human reason.

3. Theology tends to divide Christian forces because it obscures the mission of the Church. ... Perhaps in heaven we will be theologians, but on earth we are called to be evangelists.[4]

Lyman Abbott, a noted contemporary who was friendly to Moody, wrote that Moody was 'indifferent to theological theories'.[5]

Moody clearly regarded it as his mission to preach the Gospel, and his refusal to preach 'this or that doctrine' he regarded as debatable and on the periphery of the 'whosoever', does lend itself to the interpretation that he was indifferent to or opposed to doctrine.

A strong case can be built for this position. In London in 1875 an interrogator asked him for his creed. As reporters held their notebooks at the ready, Moody replied, 'It is already in print in the fifty-third chapter of Isaiah.'[6]

Moody himself told the story of a woman who came to him after a sermon and said, 'I want to be frank with you, I want you to know I do not believe in your theology.' 'My theology,' Moody exclaimed, 'I did not know I had any. I wish you would tell me what my theology is.'[7]

To these anecdotes could be added scores of statements scattered through the published versions of Moody's sermons. On the surface, many of these seem to reflect a negative attitude toward creeds, doctrines and theology.

But this is a superficial reading of Moody. What he really opposed was the dead letter of doctrine that did not also involve a living faith. He opposed reading Scripture in the light of doctrine rather than reading Scripture in the light of Calvary. He was opposed to the divisions that resulted from credal disputes. He was opposed to doctrinal correctness that was devoid of Christian compassion. He was opposed to a kind of formalism that lived on in doctrinal formularies. In short, Moody was insistent that adherence to a creed was no substitute for a personal faith in Christ; and the common bond among those who had such a faith in Christ transcended the party spirit that tended to rise out of credalism.

But for Moody it still 'makes all the difference in the world whether a man believes a truth or a lie'.[8] In his sermon on faith preached in London in 1875 and again at the New York Hippodrome in 1876, Moody spoke of faith as consisting of knowledge, assent and laying hold. He then went on so say, as he often did, that sincerity was not enough – it made all the difference in the world what one believed.[9] The same sermon was preached again within a year and, as reported in the book *New Sermons, Addresses and Prayers*, he was even more specific in warning against false ideas of God, the sincere followers of Baal, error and the folly that 'any creed is good . . . if they only believe it'. He is even critical of people who 'go wandering about without any definite belief – who don't know what they believe'.[10]

Nearly twenty-five years later, at the end of his career, Moody was saying the same thing. It was his last summer at the Northfield General Conference, in 1899, that he said:

> People have an idea now that it makes very little difference what a man believes if he is only sincere, if he is only honest in his creed. I have that question put to me many a time: 'Mr Moody, you don't think it makes any difference what a man believes if he is only sincere?' I believe it is one of the greatest lies that ever came out of the pit of hell. Why they virtually say you can believe a lie just as well as you believe the truth, if you are only earnest . . . and stick to it.[11]

In view of statements like this, it is significant that Moody did not regard evangelism as the only valid ministry. As early as 1875 he was saying that it was the work of pastors to build up and feed young converts.[12] In the summer of 1888 he told college students assembled at Northfield that what we needed was more teaching and less preaching. Too many sermons were all exhortation or directed to the unconverted. Later that summer he advised them to take a month of personal Bible study to study each of the fundamental doctrines, specifically mentioning faith, assurance, atonement, justification and sanctification.[13]

Moody hardly sounds like an evangelist for whom method had triumphed over message or for whom theology and doctrine had little significance. In fact, just because saving faith in Christ was the ultimate goal, it was important to have right doctrine. In his sermon on faith delivered in New Bedford, Massachusetts in 1895, he describes the complementary relationship as he understood it. The sermon opens with a warning that faith is not mere intellectual assent, nor is it a leap into the dark. Then he goes on to say:

> If a man should ask me up to his house for dinner tomorrow, the street would be a very good thing to take me to his house. But if I didn't get into the house, I wouldn't get any dinner. Now a creed is the road or street. It is very good as far as it goes, but if it doesn't take us to Christ it is worthless. . . . Faith [is] in a person, and that person is Christ. It isn't a creed about him, but it is himself.[14]

Moody's revivalist/evangelistic methodology was in logical and historical succession from Charles Finney

This myth is related to the one we just discussed in that it is an extension of the claim that method triumphed over message and that the conversion experience was a function of technique. Revivals were to be worked up, not prayed down. The man-made elements of revival supposedly had come to dominate in Moody, and this was in direct succession from Charles Finney. Historian William McLoughlin argued that Finney had established the theory of modern revivalism that by the proper use of means revivals could be produced at will and that the end justified the means. Moody allegedly applied Finney's principles to urban evangelism for the first time so that 'it became possible to promote city-wide interdenominational revivals at will'.[15] Bernard Weisberger takes a similar view, emphasizing the 'superdevelopment' of 'machine-made' revivals under Moody.[16]

The mainstay of McLoughlin's argument is a statement that Moody supposedly made in 1877, 'It makes no difference how you get a man to God, provided you get him there.'[17] This statement is so at odds with views expressed by Moody throughout the entire record of his ministry that it would be difficult to accept it at face value even if we did not have access to the primary source to check it out within context. But we do have access to that 'source', and, in fact, McLoughlin misuses it. The source of the 'quotation' is a reporter's account and personal analysis of meetings that were being held in the Boston Tabernacle in 1877. The context does not clearly indicate whether the statement McLoughlin quotes is actually something Moody said, or merely the reporter's analysis. Even assuming that this statement is Moody's, the reporter provides no context for the statement. And the reporter himself does not draw from the 'statement' the conclusion that McLoughlin draws, namely that the end justifies the means. Instead, he says that Scripture justifies the means, for every act he has a scriptural authority.

McLoughlin goes on to build his case on a quotation from William Hoyt Coleman, an observer of Moody's meeting in New York in 1876. The excised quote read, 'The Hippodrome is a vast business enterprise, organized and conducted by business-men, who put their money into it on business principles, for the purpose of saving souls.'[18] Aside from the fact that the quotation from Coleman does not prove that Moody thought that business technique could save souls, it is curious that McLoughlin does not quote this observer's next sentence. It reads, 'But through all the machinery vibrates the power without which it would all be useless – the power of the Holy Ghost.'[19]

The whole tenor of Moody's message and ministry, together with flawed, selective use of sources, undercuts McLoughlin's thesis that Moody took Finney's 'new measures to their next level – urban evangelism'. There are also other problems with this view. Moody readily expressed his indebtedness to contemporaries like Charles Haddon Spurgeon, C. H. Mackintosh and Henry Moorhouse. Before he came to public notice in 1873, he travelled to Great Britain three times to consult with and learn from the great evangelical leaders there. This was Moody's mode of self-instruction – seeking out leaders from whom he could learn. But there is no evidence that Moody had any direct or indirect relationship with Finney, yet Finney lived until 1875. While this is an argument from silence, and hence inconclusive, I suggest that in this case the silence is likely very significant.

There are other considerations that make a connection between Finney and Moody unlikely. As a young Christian, Moody's roots were in the prayer revival of 1857–8, a revival in which Finney and his methods played no significant part. Moody consistently rejected the idea that using the right techniques would produce revival. He eschewed in both word and practice the kind of emotionalism and high-pressure tactics that can so readily be used by evangelists to manipulate crowds. Indeed, it was the absence of such tactics that commended the work of Moody and Sankey to the Scots.[20] R. W. Dale, the leading Congregational minister in late Victorian England, attributed the apparent success of Moody and Sankey not to their methodology, but to the power of God.[21]

This is not to suggest, of course, that Moody was not innovative in his evangelistic methodology. He avoided the extremes of emotionalism, even cutting services short if he sensed things were getting out of control. He refused to be sensationalist and often expressed embarrassment over others who were. Yet he would advertise; prayer meetings would precede his campaigns; the services would be kept interesting and lively; the singing was enthusiastic; in short, the details were well-planned and thought through. But Moody knew that none of this would create a spiritual awakening in itself – if that was to happen, it would come from God.

Even Moody's use of the 'inquiry room' was totally at odds with the 'anxious bench' that Finney and his imitators had used. Potential converts would be brought to the front and seated on the anxious bench at Finney's meetings, subjected to the piercing, fierce glare of Finney's eyes and subjected as well to the unseen but very real group pressure to be converted. In contrast, Moody's inquiry room was a place where those whose spiritual concern had been heightened by the service could come for further information and counsel in a quiet setting. It was this novel use of the inquiry room as a means of nurturing seeking souls that probably first attracted young Henry Drummond to Moody.[22]

In sum, Moody looked for instruction and guidance, not in the direction of Finney, but rather to the likes of Spurgeon and Moorhouse.

Moody was a Pentecostal before Pentecostalism

North American Pentecostalism is normally traced to the first day of the twentieth century, 1 January 1901 and Charles Parham in Topeka, Kansas. Similarity between Moody's terminology in referring to the work of the Holy Spirit and the vocabulary of modern Pentecostalism has led some to suggest that he was a forerunner of the movement and that he advocated and engaged in speaking in tongues as the evidence of the Spirit's baptism. More often than not, this point is raised today in conversations among Pentecostal and non-Pentecostal evangelicals, letters to the editor in Christian periodicals and the popular press. But it is all on the basis of hearsay evidence. The connection is rarely made within scholarly literature.

The evidence for this connection is dubious. The closest link that can be established between Moody and the tongues phenomenon is a report from Sunderland, England in the fall of 1873. Moody had addressed the local YMCA on a Sunday afternoon. That evening there was a meeting at the Sunderland YMCA with speaking in tongues and prophesying. However, Moody was not at that evening meeting, and only a few weeks later Moody and Sankey were warmly received in Scotland precisely because their brand of revivalism did not cater to such phenomena. An observer at Stockton-on-Tees in early November 1873 reported:

> Another important feature was the *absence of noise* in the meetings. The experience of the past few days in Stockton will, we think, have convinced them that the best and most successful prayer meetings held in Stockton have been the quietist, reminding us of the old lady's description, 'God Almighty was so near that nobody had to shout to Him.'[23]

As for Moody's own comments on the matter, there is not a single place in the great mass of his published sermons and comments, nor in his private sermon notes, where he ever suggested that he had spoken in tongues or where he advocated speaking in tongues. And though he often spoke of the need for 'empowering for service', never once did he make a connection between that experience and tongues speaking.

On the rare occasions where he did refer to tongues in the New Testament, he hardly did so in the fashion of a glossolalist. He interpreted the 'new tongues' of Mark 16:17 as tongues that were not slanderous. On one occasion he applied Paul's prohibition of speaking in an unknown tongue to choirs that sing such fine, operatic music in church that no one understands, so that all but the select few go to sleep! On still another occasion he saw a parallel between the tongues of Acts 2 and the new eloquence and power of ministers who had experienced 'empowerment for service'.[24]

Whatever one's position on glossolalia, there is likely agreement that Moody's exegesis is seriously flawed in each of these passages. But that is not the point here. It is, rather, that no case at all can be made for Moody being a forerunner of modern Pentecostalism.

Moody was a perfectionist and espoused second blessing theology

We must pick our way through this subject very carefully lest we be guilty of the same simplistic conclusion that McLoughlin made when he declared that Finney and Moody shared the 'perfectionist belief that a truly converted Christian is free from sin and all its temptations'.[25] The facts do not support this pronouncement. Indeed, the subject is much too complex to allow for any such simple conclusion on any side of this issue.

The problem stems from the fact there were many strands of perfectionist thought in the nineteenth century. Similarly, there were, and are still today, different varieties of 'second blessing' theology. With all due respect to many personal friends within contemporary Wesleyan or 'Christian holiness' circles, it is difficult for me as a historian to evaluate their appreciation for Moody's view of 'empowerment for service'. The problem is that Wesleyans do not even agree among themselves concerning the second blessing or second work of grace, entire sanctification, sinless perfection, perfect love and related concepts. A further complication is how the Keswick movement of the last quarter of the nineteenth century fits into all this. Early Keswick tended to have perfectionistic tendencies, whereas the later Keswick tended to distance itself from those tendencies. Rather than try to sort and separate all these tangled strands, perhaps it is best simply to consider Moody's own views.

It can be said with a great deal of confidence that Moody was not a perfectionist. He was uncomfortable with the early Keswick movement on precisely this issue. But in the 1880s and 1890s, when Keswick moved toward stressing holiness of life and away from the eradication of inward sin, Moody's transatlantic connections with Keswick became closer. He even preached at the Keswick convention in 1892. There, in the presence of Keswick leaders, Moody said, 'I dare not make any professions of being holy'.[26]

Why then would anyone ever suggest that Moody was a perfectionist? Because Moody made statements that superficially sounded perfectionistic: Christ keeps us from sin day by day; Christ delivers from all sin, all appetite, all lust; the new birth takes away all sin and desire for it and gives victory.[27] While such statements sound convincing, upon closer examination, they are not.

These statements all referred to the new nature that one has by the new birth. In almost every case where Moody speaks in terms that could be interpreted as implying the possibility of sinless perfection, he also affirms within the very same context the continuance of the old Adamic nature. In fact, he would affirm that the old man was not dead and that Christ knows believers by their defects.

There is another consideration that leads to this conclusion. Though there is not a necessary relationship between postmillennialism and the various sorts of perfectionism, there is certainly a very friendly compatibility. Finney tied the two together in his thought, and it is interesting that relatively few Wesleyans of either the nineteenth or twentieth century have been attracted to premillennialism. Interestingly enough, Moody did tie his denial of perfectionism to his premillenialism![28]

Moody did reject perfectionism, but he also held a view that many Wesleyans find friendly to their cause, and that Moody's twentieth-century namesakes have found embarrassing, or at least something they would just as soon ignore.

While Moody believed that the Holy Spirit established a permanent relationship with the believer at conversion and regeneration, he also believed that something more of the Spirit was needed for effective Christian service. It was what he called the 'Holy Spirit upon us for service'. In 1871 Moody had such an experience. He seldom talked about it publicly, but when he did he described it as a filling, a baptism or an anointing that came on him when he was in a cold state. His selfish ambitions in preaching were surrendered, and he then received power by which to do his work for Christ.[29]

In his frequent expositions of the topic, surrender to God's will with the consequent empowering for service was the controlling and almost exclusive theme. Some of Moody's contemporaries did not accept the validity or necessity of that kind of experience, and others interpreted such experiences as an eradication of the old nature or as effecting an entire sanctification. Moody even alluded to those who tried to straighten him out on the subject. But he knew what he had experienced, and he found it quite compatible with biblical terminology.

Moody was a dispensationalist

Moody is frequently depicted as a dispensationalist, but this conclusion is based on assumption rather than argument. After all, he was clearly a primillennialist (no one disagrees with that point), and in the last quarter of the nineteenth century it was often assumed that premillennialists were *ipso facto* dispensationalists. Further, various Plymouth Brethren were significant influences on young Moody. Dispensationalists beyond the Brethren fold were close associates of Moody and frequently spoke at the Northfield conferences. In fact, the celebrated C. I. Scofield took over Moody's church in East Northfield at Moody's request, and served as pastor there from 1895 to 1902.

But was Moody a dispensationalist? The answer to that question depends on how clearly we expect him to articulate his views to qualify as a dispensationalist. One finds only general dispensational themes in his messages. For example, Moody claimed to follow a literal interpretation of prophecy and believed there would be a regathering of the Jewish people. This included the restoration of the nation of Israel and the literal fulfilment of promises with reference to her. On occasion he emphasized the Jewishness of the millennial kingdom. He would preach that the believer should expect the coming of Christ to be sudden, unexpected and secret. He even said that Christ would come to take his bride, the church, out of the world before he came in judgement. All of these ideas have clear dispensational overtones.

But it is not quite that simple. Usually his sermons contained only vague, general affirmations of premillennialism. Moody nowhere refers to a pre- or post-tribulational rapture, nor to a seven-year tribulation, as normally expected of dispensationalists.

It is especially interesting to note Moody's attitudes toward the debates over prophecy near the end of his life. In the mid-1880s and the 1890s two prominent and highly respected premillennialists, Robert Cameron and Nathaniel West, began to question the dispensational doctrine of the any-moment pre-tribulational rapture. West drew upon the work of Samuel P. Tregelles, a notable Old Testament scholar and leader among the British Plymouth Brethren.

In 1893 West publicly attacked the any-moment secret rapture teaching, and the more or less solid front that American premillennialism had presented began to fragment. Moody's response to this situation was to say that '*when* His coming will be, we don't know. The true attitude of every child of God is just to be waiting and watching.' Beyond that, Moody did not get involved in the details of the debate. He had no reason to since he had apparently not set forth a detailed chronology of future events.

During these debates, Moody continued to preach an any-moment return, but by 1897 a new note had crept into his preaching, a note that reflected his concerns about the controversy raging in premillennial ranks. Preaching to a congregation in Boston's Tremont Temple he warned, 'Don't criticize if our watches don't agree about the time that we know he is coming.' Then he even held out an olive branch to the postmillennialists and said, 'We will not have division.' Though he continued to preach his brand of an any-moment return in terms that were both vague and somewhat dispensational in tone, he would warn:

> I believe truth has suffered more from its so-called friends than from others. We have been making out a programme to tell us what is going to happen, and one who does that has a big job. . . . When you come to make out a programme, I differ, I don't know! I don't think anyone knows what is going to happen![30]

Was Moody a dispensationalist? Probably vaguely so, but hardly with a clarity and conviction that would make most dispensationalists then or now happy. Perhaps all of us, regardless of our prophetic views, would do well to emulate some of the prophetic agnosticism and humility that Moody expressed toward the end of his life.

Moody rejected the substitutionary theory of the atonement in favour of the moral influence theory of the atonement

One very significant book tries to make this case: James Findlay's definitive scholarly biography *Dwight L. Moody: American Evangelist 1837–1899* (University of Chicago Press, 1969). While a helpful biography in many ways, this study is less reliable as a guide to Moody's theology.

The issue is really quite simple. Findlay does not understand Moody correctly because he does not understand the essential differences between the moral influence theory of the atonement and the penal substitutionary theory of the atonement.

To a point, Findlay correctly describes the two views. In the moral influence theory the stress is laid on the manifestation of God's love for sinners in the total mission and work of Christ, including his obedience in death. The moral influence of his life and death breaks down the sinner's opposition to God. The penal substitutionary view has its primary effect on God the Father in that Christ's death in the sinner's place satisfies the wrath of God and releases humankind from the demand of the law that sinners be punished.

But Findlay then goes on to say that the essential difference between the two theories is the view of God set forth by each. The penal substitutionary theory is said to view God as a stern, wrathful judge and the moral influence theory is said to view God as tender and loving. From this Findlay concludes that Moody held to the moral influence theory since he was, in fact, convinced of the love of God as revealed in Christ's death on the cross.

Here's the issue: is the love of God the *crux interpretum* between these two theories? Or to put the question differently, is a God whose holiness demands satisfaction necessarily any less a God of love than a God who manifests his love through Christ's example? The answer to both questions is 'no'. For Anselm, the first theologian to clearly and systematically spell out the substitutionary view in his work *Cur Deus Homo?*, God's love was the starting point, the source of salvation. The substitutionary atonement in the person of his Son had its source in God's loving grace. Later Protestant theologians accepted and refined the Anselmic substitutionary view. This was Moody's view.

What Findlay failed to understand is that in the moral influence theory the essential nature and effect of the atonement is to be found in its subjective *a*ffect on sinners – its moral influence on them. In the penal substitutionary view the essential nature and effect of the atonement is to be found in its objective accomplishment and *e*ffect on God – satisfaction of the righteous demands of a holy God. Had Findlay understood this to be the difference between the two theories, I am confident he would have correctly interpreted Moody.

Moody's view of the significance of Christ's death is found everywhere in his sermons, but nowhere more clearly than in two sermons that are really one, usually preached on successive evenings.[31] In them he traces the 'line of blood', first through the Old Testament, then through the New Testament. He focuses on key moments in the history of redemption such as the shedding of blood in the provision of the skin coverings for Adam and Eve, the difference between the offerings of Cain and Abel, the sacrificial substitute for Isaac on Mount Moriah, the Passover, the Levitical sacrificial system, and the prophetic significance of Isaiah 53. When he comes to the New Testament, he sees this all fulfilled in Christ and spends considerable time expounding on the sacrificial, substitutionary nature of Christ's death.

Throughout this two-part sermon the key words and concepts are penalty, substitution, sacrifice, blood, satisfaction and love. At one point Moody alluded to his Unitarian upbringing (Unitarians held to a moral influence theory) and confessed that 'there was a time when I didn't believe in the substitution and the blood'. It is significant that Unitarians and Universalists were almost vitriolic in their opposition to Moody. They were adamantly opposed to his view of the atonement, having correctly understood him to preach a penal, substitutionary view.[32]

Moody was an incipient theological liberal, or a fundamentalist
In the last quarter of the nineteenth century a number of trends converged to challenge the traditional doctrines of the Christian faith. The umbrella term commonly used to cover this convergence is 'liberalism'. The streams that converged to produce liberalism were Unitarianism, transcendentalism, the evolutionary worldview, radical higher criticism, and philosophical idealism. The full-blown result of this convergence was a liberalism that viewed the Bible as essentially a human book; accepted a moral influence theory of the atonement; emphasized the immanence of God nearly to the point of pantheism; insisted on the essential worth of human nature; and preached the universal Fatherhood of God and brotherhood of man and the Social Gospel.

This convergence was pretty well completed in the first two decades of the twentieth century, and with that came a polarization between the liberals and those who soon came to be known as the fundamentalists. And with that came the question, 'Where would Mr Moody stand?', a question asked in no less a liberal journal than *The Christian Century* in its issue of 12 July 1923. This editorial brought to public attention a debate that had been brewing for some time: Who were the true heirs of Moody? Was it the YMCA in which Moody had early on been such a formative influence and the Northfield schools he had founded, both of which were steadily moving down the road toward liberalism? Or was it Moody Bible Institute? Would Moody have stood with the liberals or the fundamentalists?

The Christian Century's answer was unmistakable: not with what it perceived to be the fundamentalist stance of the

Institute. Even Moody's younger son Paul argued within the pages of this same liberal voice that his father was for his day a liberal and that if 'he were living today [1923] . . . he would be . . . more in sympathy with the men who, like Fosdick, are preaching what he loved to spread – the love of God and the power of Christ – than with those who are attempting to persecute them because they will not substitute certain shibboleths'.[33]

That such a question should even be asked, let alone require an answer, might seem strange in light of what we have seen about the conservative evangelical theology implicit in Moody's preaching. Still, there was some justification for the question. Moody was a man of broad spirit. Lyman Abbott rightly lauded him for his catholicity of spirit. Within a few days of Moody's death, liberal Old Testament scholar, George Adam Smith, bemoaned the fact that 'we have lost not only one of the strong-est personalities of our time, but a man who was more able than any other to act as a reconciler of our present divisions'.[34] Moody's close personal relationship with Henry Drummond and his invitations to higher critics such as Smith and William Rainey Harper to speak at Northfield were further reasons why these questions emerged.

However, the literature evoked by this controversy is more interesting for the light that it sheds on the fundamentalist–modernist controversies of the 1920s than for what it reveals about where Moody would have stood. Often the debate boiled down to the recollections of a Paul Moody or a George Adam Smith against the recollections of an R. A. Torrey, a former associate of Moody, first superintendent of the Institute and then later Dean of the Bible Institute of Los Angeles, and Charles Blanchard, a former pastor of Moody Memorial Church and longtime president of Wheaton College. For every assertion that Moody associated with liberals and invited them to Northfield because he recognized within these men genuine Christian faith, one can find counter-assertions that Moody invited these men in ignorance and regretted these invitations after he knew better. The debate proved little more than that both sides wanted to claim Moody's mantle as his true heirs.

The Christian Century's question remains unanswered in the final analysis because it was the wrong question. The polarization between liberals and conservatives was much more pronounced in the 1920s than it was in Moody's time. Although the opposing forces were already pulling at Moody in the 1890s, it is difficult, probably impossible, to determine precisely where Moody would have stood in the 1920s. That his theology would have been essentially unchanged seems to be a reasonable conclusion. But what his relationships with and attitudes toward the two poles would have been is a moot question. In fact, had Moody lived and remained active for another ten or fifteen years, perhaps the whole relationship between liberalism and conservatism would have taken a different course.

When we reflect on this man and his work, what stands out are the great centring themes of his preaching and ministry:

- His focus on the essentials of the Gospel.
- His profound understanding of God's love, and that love must also motivate all that we do for God.
- His understanding that neither his lack of formal education disqualified him nor his considerable energies and skills qualified him for God's work – he rightly understood that his strength for the work to which God had called him came from God himself.
- His consistency and common sense in serving the cause of Christ.
- His broad, mediating spirit and influence in the midst of controversy.

May God give us more men and women like Mr Moody to carry on the work which he began.

2

D. L. MOODY:
MORE THAN AN EVANGELIST

Lyle W. Dorsett

Dwight L. Moody is remembered as an evangelist. During his lifetime the press and churches focused attention on his evangelistic preaching, the large crowds that attended his meetings and the extraordinary number of people who committed or recommitted their lives to Jesus Christ at these services. His biographers have helped reinforce this image. John Pollock's widely read popular portrait of Mr Moody is titled *Moody: A Biographical Portrait of the Pacesetter in Mass Evangelism* and James F. Findlay Jr's scholarly biography is *Dwight L. Moody: American Evangelist, 1837–1899*. Both authors celebrate Moody as essentially an evangelist.

Depicting Moody as an evangelist is certainly valid. Indeed, few men in modern history can be so accurately labelled with the title 'evangelist' in the context in which it is lifted up by the Apostle Paul in Ephesians ch. 4. Nevertheless, Mr Moody saw himself rather differently than his contemporaries and modern church historians. He saw himself from a wider perspective and with a markedly different sense of his major contributions.

Throughout the mature years of his ministry D. L. Moody emphasized 'this one thing I do', referring to God's call on his life to work with souls.[1] It is apparent from his ministry, however, that he was referring to a call that encompassed the healing and nurture of souls as well as the rescue of souls, or evangelism. Moody took the view that Christ's great commission calls us to make disciples, not mere converts (Matt. 28.18–20). Consequently, he laboured incessantly to help people grow up into strong, reproducing disciples, and he strove to equip people to become full-time workers in this broader disciple-making work of rescuing, healing and nurturing souls.

Mr Moody loved his broader ministry and he called it 'the work'. In one of his last letters – written a month before he died – he referred to both the formal and non-formal educational programmes he founded, which he believed were among his most significant enterprises: 'The work is sweeter now than ever, and I think I have some streams started that will flow on forever. What a joy to be in the harvest field and have a hand in God's work!'[2] In the same vein he told his son, Will, that the schools 'are the best pieces of work I have ever done'.[3]

The purpose of this essay is to present a glimpse of Dwight L. Moody's vision beyond evangelism. I want to look at Moody's broader ministry because I believe that Moody's goals are still relevant to the revival of the Christian faith and the recovery of vibrant church life throughout the world.

The rhetoric that Moody used by the early 1870s reveals a concern for souls. In fact, he was concerned for the entire souls of people. He manifested what I can only describe as 'a passion for souls' which is the title of my biography of D. L. Moody. As an evangelist he was mightily interested in rescuing souls, but equally important to this man, born and raised in rural poverty, was seeing souls healed and nurtured so that they could grow up, go forth and reproduce their kind. It is important to understand that, unlike many evangelists, Moody had no interest in converts *per se*. Seeing healthy reproducing disciples was his goal. His passion centred on the whole person. Therefore he became singularly unimpressed with statistics and always concentrated on follow-up work with those who were prayed for out of the large crowds. He stressed that the primary ministry only begins with preaching to large gatherings. The crucial work, he argued, is 'personal work'.[4]

Moody's approach was a marked change from that employed by Charles G. Finney. Moody eschewed the 'anxious bench' because he did not want people responding to an evangelist's pressure. Instead, the Massachusetts native offered an 'inquiry room' where those who heard his message were invited to go if they had questions, desired counsel or felt a need for prayer. In the inquiry room 'the personal work' began in earnest.

The journal of Jane McKinnon, housed in the library of Yale Divinity School, is an important document for understanding some of Moody's goals and methodology. Jane McKinnon's husband gave his life to Jesus Christ under the ministry of Mr Moody. Eventually this Scotsman and his wife followed the American throughout his travels in the United Kingdom. They became important members of Moody's entourage and they were frequently employed as volunteer counsellors in the inquiry rooms and other modes of follow up. Mrs McKinnon kept detailed notes of Moody's instructions and 'the personal work' in a large journal. After Mr Moody died she had the journal typed and gave a copy to Mrs D. L. Moody. This document is a gold-mine of information and worthy of further exploration.

According to McKinnon, Moody would provide training sessions for volunteers who would help him in the inquiry rooms.

> Take time with each person, Moody insisted. Listen to them and listen carefully – both to them and to the Holy Spirit. Look in the inquirer's eyes. Stay with him. There probably will be a line of people waiting to be served, but don't let them take you from your post. They will wait until you are finished. And if they don't wait, pay no attention. God has given you this soul and she or he needs your full attention.[5]

I am struck at how Moody's approach differed from Billy Sunday's. The famous baseball player and evangelist would urge people, after his sermons, to 'Come forward and shake the hand of Billy Sunday if you intend to live for Jesus Christ'. People would crowd to the front and some later remarked that it broke their hearts when he would treat their decision – the most important in their life – in a casual manner. At times men and women recalled that they would come forward, offer their hand and he would be looking at the next person in line before he let go of them.[6]

Unlike Billy Sunday and many evangelists who speak to large crowds, Moody insisted on the personal touch. He continually stressed that each soul was unique and precious to God and must be ministered to in that way.

How did Moody learn this when so many others before and

after him never caught on? I think he learned it during the American Civil War. It is important to understand that Moody had no formal theological and ministerial training. At most he had four years of elementary education. This was both an advantage and disadvantage. There was no institutional mould in which he had been shaped. He had no mentor who passed on a systematic theology, a method of hermeneutics or homiletical style. Except for a few godly people who taught him to love the Lord, pray and study the Bible, plus the books of George Müller and sermons of Charles Spurgeon, Moody was on his own. Early in his ministry he became a Civil War chaplain. And it was in the tent hospitals where he learned the importance of personal work. Moody stayed near the front lines of the battles. He worked around the clock listening to wounded and dying men. There he learned the fears and hopes in men's hearts. Kneeling by the cots or floor pallets of dying soldiers, Confederate and Union, talking to them about their souls, listening to their stories, hearing their confessions and trying to lead them into the presence of Jesus Christ became his school. There he learned that some men were hearty souls who were ready to meet the One they had loved and served. Others were weak souls who had never experienced healing, revealed no true relationship with Christ or had only a passing acquaintance with him. Why did some soldiers have assurance of salvation, whereas others said they were Christian but had no confidence about their ultimate destiny?

Dwight Moody grew convinced that the differences he observed could be attributed to one thing – care for the soul. Some men never surrendered their lives to Christ, but, alas, many were mere converts who never received spiritual healing and nurture. The hardy ones, on the other hand, had been cared for along the way by soul physicians who offered holistic care.

Moody took what he learned in the tent hospitals and applied it throughout his ministry until he died in December 1899. From the lay training programmes to the inquiry rooms, he led the people from listening and prayer to carefully making certain that each soul had a church with a pastor or lay leader who would purposively follow up; to these things he dedicated much of his time.

Concomitant with this goal, Moody had a burning drive to prepare the next generation to do the work of soul care. From his earliest days of ministry he worked with indigent children in Chicago. Unlike many church workers, he found favour with the city's poorest children. He led countless girls and boys to Christ and many grew up to become reproducing Christian disciples. Always a man with a passion for young people, he tamed many of the impoverished and unruly when other outreach attempts failed. Moody's success resulted from many factors – his prayers, God's anointing and his keen sense of calling. Equally important, of course, was the fact that Moody had been one of them as a child. He understood their needs and desires.

The street urchins Moody reached had almost no attention span. They had never experienced discipline. When someone tried to bring them into a traditional Sunday School they would totally disrupt it within ten minutes. When they were introduced to a worship service on Sunday morning they would drive the congregation out with their body odour, language and wild antics. Mr Moody rented facilities and gradually broke them in like wild horses. He would bring them in, speak to them for five minutes and then let them wrestle for a few minutes. They would then sing a song to be followed by another stretch of rowdiness.

Soon Christian leaders discovered that Moody had the genius to develop a programme that worked rather than go down fighting using a model culturally unfit for those he sought to help. Astute observers also saw that Moody had an eye and heart for the younger generation. And once again, Moody's own deprived and tumultuous background served him well to reach the next generation.

D. L. Moody typified many Americans and British people in the late Victorian age. Like hundreds of thousands of people, he grew up in a rural area but migrated to the burgeoning cities to find fame and fortune. Most of these teeming masses had little education. If they found some advantages in urban life, the social problems that plagued them were legion. Civility, morality and the nuclear family fell into disarray. Crime, sexual promiscuity, alcoholism and morphine and opium addiction were rampant. Who could reach these people with the Gospel?

Who could offer them holistic soul care within a culturally relevant context?

As Moody and other Christians discovered, college-trained ministers and city missionaries failed to reach these people, hard as they tried. The problem was that the well-meaning, educated élite could not relate to the new urban populations. They could not even speak their language. From Moody's perspective the solution to the problem was clear. Take some of the younger men and women who had emigrated to the city and given their lives to Christ, and see if they had a calling to care for souls. If so, a training centre needed to be established to take in people with little formal schooling, teach them the English Bible, basic doctrine and theology, and then train them to do evangelism and personal work. They also had to be encouraged to be tent makers who were willing to earn their own living to support their ministries.

To this end Moody, with God's help, set several streams in motion. He drafted a Christian professional educator, Emma Dryer, to start a school in Chicago that became Chicago Bible Institute, known today as Moody Bible Institute. From its inception men and women in the Midwest were taken in and trained to become urban missionaries. Meanwhile, back in the community of his birth, Northfield, Massachusetts, Mr Moody launched a similar school for young women called the Northfield Bible Training School.

Both Bible training schools became immediately successful in attracting and training students and getting them placed in soul care ministries; but Moody's efforts on behalf of the younger generation did not stop there. He and his son, Will, partnered with several wealthy businessmen, as well as male and female philanthropists. Under the Moodys' direction a college preparatory school for girls, the Northfield Seminary for Young Women, began in 1879, to be followed two years later by the Mount Hermon Boys' School located just a few miles away. These two institutions served socially and economically disadvantaged youth from the north-eastern United States, plus some able teenagers from foreign mission fields as far away as India and Africa. These foreign nationals, as well as the Americans, worked hard at the school and their farming, cooking, cleaning and sewing labours were supplemented by wealthy donors who shared the Moody vision.

Moody did more than equip city workers and place young people in college preparatory schools; he determined to encourage and help nurture a generation of college men and women to take the gospel and personal work to the Americas and the uttermost parts of the world. To this end, in 1880 he began a series of summer conferences in the grounds of the Northfield schools in Massachusetts. College students from all over the United States went there by train, horse and on foot. Some found beds in dormitories but most of the young people slept in tents or on bed rolls under the trees in the surrounding hills. Mr Moody brought the best inspirational speakers and Bible teachers he could find, including A. T. Pierson, Henry Drummond, A. J. Gordon, G. Campbell Morgan, I. B. Meyer, A. A. Bonar and Hudson Taylor. By the 1890s college people came from Great Britain, Europe and many parts of Asia to Moody's summer conferences. This movement was a precursor to the late twentieth-century InterVarsity student conferences. These Northfield conferences served as sparkplugs to ignite the souls of young people to give their lives to promulgating the good news of Jesus Christ.

The streams of the Chicago and Northfield schools still flow on. Indeed, only the Northfield Bible Training School is gone, closing a few years after its founder's death. And if these institutions are impressive, equally important are some other rivers of Gospel waters that continue to flow from D. L. Moody's Spirit-inspired visions. When Moody could not find printed material to use in his training programmes and schools, he urged his brother-in-law, Fleming H. Revell, to resign his position as a drugstore clerk and begin a Christian publishing business. In 1869 Revell took the challenge and very soon thereafter found himself overseeing a lucrative periodical and book company that annually published a growing list of books by well-known Christian authors. Leading the author list, of course, was D. L. Moody, always the company's top-selling author until the twentieth century. Revell, thanks originally to Moody's help, also published books by such lights as A. J. Gordon, George Müller and D. W. Whittle.

Fleming H. Revell's publishing house is still turning out

impressive lists of books by Christian authors. But so is a second publishing venture that Mr Moody personally undertook in 1895. In the summer of 1894 Moody had the idea that inexpensive paperback books – like the popular 'dime novels' of the time – needed to be produced so that books could be mass produced and placed in the hands of Christian workers, Sunday school teachers and prison inmates. Moody's brother-in-law, however, predicted that such a venture would fail. There was, he believed, only a small market and it would never produce more than meagre profits. Never one to be deterred from what he saw as a vision from God, Moody hitched his paperback scheme to the Chicago Bible Institute.

Eventually the Chicago Bible Colportage Association was organized. Hundreds of Bible Institute students sold thousands of paperbacks door-to-door and church-to-church for many years. This vision led to publication of hundreds of titles, the promotion of established and new authors, the spread of Christian teaching to jails, prisons, churches, schools and homes. Today this venture, over a century old, is Moody Press, a division of Moody Bible Institute. The rivers flow on.

Thus Dwight L. Moody was much 'more than an evangelist'. His determination to care for souls through personal work is worthy of our consideration in an age when we tend to measure the success of our ministry by numbers. Furthermore, his investment in young people is the only way to insure that the rivers of our work will flow on long after we have departed this earth.

3

THE GREAT TURNING POINT IN THE LIFE OF D. L. MOODY

Don Sweeting

If anyone hopes to understand nineteenth-century British and American evangelicalism, it is necessary to study the life and ministry of D. L. Moody. Apart from Billy Graham, he is, as the 1953 *Encyclopaedia Britannica* referred to him, 'the greatest modern evangelist'.[1] This energetic man dominated the Christian scene of his day. His Chicago associate, Emma Dryer, rightly referred to him as 'divinely equipped flying artillery on life's battlefield'.[2]

But I also have a great personal interest in the life of D. L. Moody. My grandfather was converted through the ministry of Bethany Hall and Tent Hall in Glasgow, Scotland. These gospel halls started as a result of Moody's Scotland campaign in 1873. That makes Moody my spiritual great-great-grandfather.

Moody's meetings there were held in a large tent located on the Glasgow Green. For many of the converts these non-denominational meeting halls became a primary source of Christian fellowship and nurture. The halls were known both for serving the city's poor and for engaging in aggressive evangelism.[3]

After my grandfather emigrated to the United States, he advised his three sons to 'Go to Mr Moody's school in Chicago'. My dad and mom both graduated from Moody Bible Institute. I was the first of their children to attend, not because I was coerced, but because I thought it would be a great place to learn how to be a full-time Christian. And it was. My favourite teacher from those years was Stan Gundry. He awakened in me a love for theology. And my pastor at the time was a first-rate

Bible teacher named Warren Wiersbe! Both of these outstanding Christian leaders represent the best of Moody's legacy for the church today, and I am pleased to join them in this symposium on his life and work. In this essay, I would like to focus on what I call 'The Great Turning Point in the Life of D. L. Moody'.[4]

Most of us have more than one great defining moment in our lives. That was also true for Moody. One thinks, for example, of such key events as his conversion to Christianity in 1855. His decision to give up the business world to become an independent city missionary in 1861 was another turning point. His 1867 transformation under the preaching of Henry Moorhouse, through which Moody came to a deeper understanding of the love of God, was also pivotal.

Without overlooking the significance of these events, however, it is still accurate to speak of a great turning point in Moody's life. That turning point surrounds the events of the Chicago fire of 1871. From a human point of view, it was a time of personal catastrophe. Moody lost everything he had worked for in Chicago since arriving there in 1856. But from a divine point of view, it was a refining experience that launched Moody into a worldwide ministry.

Moody before the fire

Think of what he had built up by that time. It all started with a ministry to impoverished children in the run-down area of Chicago known as 'The Sands'. Those were the days when he was called 'Crazy Moody'. He boldly went where few Christian ministries dared to go – to the poor and destitute. Many churches were too proper to take his students in. So Moody started his own Christian meetings in a saloon. In 1858, he organized the North Market Hall Sabbath School. The work grew and others noticed his success. In 1863, he was appointed 'city missionary' of the YMCA. Whereas churches were reluctant to take the 'unqualified Moody' on, the YMCA gave him an open door.

Converts from Moody's ministry wanted a church that spoke to them on their level. By 1864 Moody had helped organize the Illinois Street Church for his followers. It was, in a way, the Willow Creek of his day (another youth ministry gone big!). Only it was a youth ministry in the inner city!

During the American Civil War, Moody also managed to work with soldiers of both armies, particularly those located in Chicago's Camp Douglas. It mattered not to him whether they were Northern troops getting ready for battle or Southern prisoners of war.

By 1865, Moody had become vice-president of the Chicago Sunday School Union. A year later he was elected president of the Chicago YMCA and was valued for his extraordinary fund-raising abilities. He also preached in the YMCA's Farwell Hall on Sunday evenings to a crowd of about 1800 young men. In his spare time he started groups like the Yokefellows, composed of men who systematically prayed for areas of the city and then went door-to-door distributing evangelistic literature. He also took occasional meetings outside of Chicago in Wisconsin, Michigan and Illinois. All in all, Moody had administrative duties on some ten to twelve different committees. He became known to many in the city as both a social organizer and an evangelist. He was, as biographer John Pollock called him, 'a dynamic Jack-of-all-trades'.[5] Moody's popularity increased to the point that some were even urging him to run for Congress – a proposition that held little appeal to him.

Christian business leaders in Chicago such as John Farwell so appreciated Moody's city work that he and others built the Moody family a brand-new, fully furnished home located on State Street. It even had an indoor bathroom!

ALL WAS NOT WELL

Despite all of the apparent successes, though, all was not well. Moody was spreading himself too thin. He had a difficult time saying 'No' to ministry opportunities that came his way. He was also drying up spiritually. Biographers such as Lyle Dorsett have noted that by the late 1860s Moody appeared to be on the brink of emotional and spiritual collapse.[6] He was on a ministry treadmill that was only speeding up. The symptoms of burnout were all there – increasing forgetfulness, double-booking, too many affairs to keep in order and occasional public out-bursts of temper.

By 1868, one doctor recommended that Moody and his wife go on a vacation to Great Britain for a break. Moody followed the doctor's advice and went. While there, he was refreshed and challenged by interaction with numerous British evangelical leaders. But after meeting and observing the great London Baptist pastor, C. H. Spurgeon, Moody felt he had to try to match Spurgeon's productivity and ambitious schedule! Spurgeon, Moody noted, preached five nights per week and also published three sermons weekly. When he returned to Chicago, his pace only increased.

On top of all this, biographers have observed that Moody at the time was stuck between two visions – one to be a social organizer, the other to be an evangelist. As gifted as he was, he could not continue doing both well. In fact, something inside told him that he was being called to concentrate on preaching and evangelism, even though he fought against it.[7]

CHICAGO IN 1871

By 1871, all was not well in Chicago either. While it was known as the 'City of Opportunity' and the 'Empire City of the West', and while it had the advantage of being a key port city and the heart of America's new vast railroad network, Chicago had a hard time keeping up with its explosive growth.[8] In 1860, Chicago's population was around 112,000. By 1871, it had already reached 300,000 people.[9] Immigrants were pouring into the city.

Pre-fire Chicago was sometimes referred to as 'the City of Pine'. Chicago had 55 miles of pine block streets, and 651 miles of wooden sidewalks. Ships in the river were made of wood. Bridges were wooden. Most of the buildings were wooden – even those that sported a marble exterior often had false fronts. Fire and building codes were routinely ignored. In an article on 1 September 1871, *The Chicago Tribune* deplored the city's 'miles of fire traps, pleasing to the eye, looking substantial, but all sham and shingles'.[10]

To make matters worse, 1871 brought one of the worst droughts in recent memory. There was only one inch of rain between 3 July and 8 October. Chicago's small fire force of 185 firemen, and 17 horse-drawn steam engines had to cope with fires breaking out all summer long. By the first week of October, the five-ton bell in the tower of the Cook County Courthouse sounded as often as seven times a day.

THE NIGHT OF THE FIRE

No one knows for sure how the Chicago fire started. Historians debate whether it was the fault of Mrs O'Leary and her cow that knocked over the kerosene lamp in her barn, or whether it was her hired hand, Dennis 'Peg Leg' Sullivan. Upon investigation, both maintained their innocence!

The great fire broke out on Sunday evening, 8 October. Flames were first noticed at 8:45 p.m. For some reason, probably due to exhaustion from battling other blazes, the fire departments were slow to respond. Flames moved northward rapidly. They jumped from homes to saloons, to shanties and then to the downtown business district. As the evening wore on, the wind picked up, some say to 60 miles per hour, blowing flaming brands and sparks high into the air. The Chicago River proved to be no barrier against these flaming winds. As the fire gathered strength, some observers said the walls of flame reached up to 300 feet high. The heat became so intense that it melted iron and steel. As city officials realized the magnitude of the blaze, fire companies from as far away as Milwaukee and Cincinnati were called in.[11]

That same evening Moody and Ira D. Sankey were conducting a meeting at the new Farwell Hall with a capacity crowd of about 2500. Moody preached. Sankey played the organ and sang. As he closed the service with a song, Sankey recalled that his voice was drowned out by the loud noise of fire engines rushing past. They could hear the great city bell calling out a general alarm.

When Moody left Farwell Hall, he crossed the river to head for his home to be with Emma and his two small children. At first it appeared that the fire would be localized, but as the hours passed, they got a knock on the door. The police urged them to flee for their lives.

By this time there was even more commotion in the city streets. Emma quickly dressed the children in two of everything, and said to them, 'if you will not scream or cry, I'll show you a sight you will never forget'.[12]

The couple grabbed a few valuables from their State Street home to take with them. His wife begged him to save a portrait of Moody that had been recently painted by a friend. At this suggestion, D. L. laughed in disbelief. 'Take my own picture? That would be a joke. Suppose I meet some friends in the same trouble as our selves and they say, "Hullo Moody, glad you have escaped. What's that you've saved and cling to so affectionately?" Wouldn't it sound well to reply, "Oh, I've got my own portrait!" ' As it turned out, someone cut the painting out of the frame anyway and it was loaded with a few other things in the pram.[13]

Moody had arranged for a friend to take his family by horse and carriage to spend the night in a northern suburb at the Spaffords' house. He would not see them again until the next day, and surely he was worried and anxious to know whether they made it through the mad panic of the Chicago streets.[14]

As the night wore on, Moody also fled north. Sankey found safety by himself in a rowing boat on Lake Michigan. The fire then raged on through the city. When the flames eventually reached the city's water pump house, it burned too and Chicago lost its water supply for fighting the fire.

The aftermath

The fire burned on until the next day. When the winds finally died down and the fire burned itself out, Chicago looked something like Atlanta after Sherman's infamous march. It was devastated. The fire scorched three and a half square miles. Eighteen thousand buildings were destroyed. Fifty churches and missions were burned to the ground and around 300 people had died. Over 100,000 were homeless. Monday's *Chicago Evening Journal* summarized the great catastrophe.

> All the principal hotels, all the public buildings, all the banks, all the newspaper offices, all the places of amusements, nearly all the great business edifices, nearly all the railroad depots, the water works, the gas works, many churches and thousands of private residences and stores have been consumed. The proud, noble, magnificent Chicago of yesterday is today a mere shadow of what it was.[15]

The same could be said of D. L. Moody's work. Everything he had laboured for was now gone. The fire destroyed the YMCA building, including Farwell Hall. This was the hall for which Moody had raised money. It was one of his preaching homes. More than that, the Chicago building was the YMCA's showpiece in North America.

The Illinois Street Church was now gone. And with the city's evacuation, the church's workers were scattered too far abroad to reorganize. Moody's house was gone too.

Providence and breakthroughs

The fire was a devastating blow to D. L. Moody. It put a complete stop to everything he had been doing. His treadmill of ministry suddenly came to a halt. Like thousands of Chicagoans, he surely asked why all of this had to happen. The answers were slow in coming.

We, on the other hand, have the perspective of time to help us see through the smoke. Christians affirm that God is providentially involved in the events of history. We do not always see God's plan clearly, but there are times when we catch a glimpse of it.

Taking the long view, secular historians have concluded that the great Chicago fire had a transforming effect upon the city itself. Donald Miller writes that from 1871 on, Chicagoans 'would date their lives with two simple three-word phrases – "before the fire" and "after the fire". The Chicago holocaust marked the end of an old order and the beginning of a new order for the city.'[16] It would be the same with D. L. Moody. The fire marked a great turning point in his ministry. Consider some of the changes that took place in Moody's life as a result of the Chicago fire.

New freedom and new concentration

First of all, the fire freed him from his previous obligations in Chicago and enabled him to focus on his new call to preach elsewhere. As someone said, the ropes that bound him to Chicago were now cut. It was God who cut the ropes. While Moody would help in the relief work, and in raising up a new North Side Tabernacle, he no longer felt obligated to be in Chicago. He himself asserted that the fire was THE event which caused him to decide to leave the city.[17]

After the fire Moody talked about the importance of two words – he would urge his listeners to 'consecrate and concentrate'. 'Consecrate your life to God', he would say. 'Concentrate your life upon some one thing and it will cut a channel so deep that your influence will be felt.'[18]

Until now, Moody had been moving in many different directions at one time. He was pastor, Sunday school superintendent, relief worker, president of the YMCA, president of the State Sunday School Association; he was a conference speaker, a moderator, money raiser and finally an evangelist. But now he was free to focus.

Moody's close friend, the retired Major D. W. Whittle said that after the fire D. L. 'lost interest in everything except the preaching of Christ and working for souls. He determined . . . to be free from all entanglements in the rebuilding of his church and Farwell Hall.'[19]

New urgency in preaching

Another change that came with the fire was a new urgency in his preaching. On the night of the fire, Moody preached on the words of Pilate, 'What then shall I do with Jesus which is called Christ?' He spoke to one of the largest crowds ever assembled at Farwell Hall. Moody concluded his sermon with what he referred to as one of the biggest blunders in his life. He told the crowd that they would have a week to decide for Christ. Then, in an ironic twist, as the flames were already spreading, Sankey closed the service by singing 'Today the Saviour Calls'.

Moody never saw that audience again. Some of them probably did not survive the night. In retrospect, he said, 'I want to tell you of one lesson I learned that night: . . . that is, when I preach, I press Christ upon the people then and there and try to bring them to a decision on the spot.'[20]

Whether he was speaking to one person or to ten thousand, Moody would from then on attempt to lead his audience to settle the matter of their eternal destiny without delay. Lovingly, and now urgently, he called for a decision.

New power for ministry

Joseph Stowell, president of Moody Bible Institute, refers to the two fires burning in Chicago in 1871. The one destroyed the city and was eventually contained. The other burned in Moody's heart and could not be contained.[21] The fire in Moody's heart that Stowell refers to is sometimes called 'Moody's personal Pentecost'. It took place shortly after the city fire.

For some time, Moody had been praying for a new Spirit-given empowerment for his ministry. In June of 1871, two women in his congregation told him that they were praying that the Lord would give Moody 'the baptism of the Holy Ghost and of fire'. At first Moody regarded their prayers as presumptuous and extreme. In time, however, he began to yearn for power from the Holy Spirit. He then agreed to meet with the two women for prayer on Friday afternoons. By September, Moody was desperate for a divine touch. The Chicago fire only intensified his longing and threw him completely upon the grace and mercy of God.

While visiting New York City in December of that year to raise money for the Chicago fire-relief work, Moody was walking down a prominent thoroughfare, praying, when an overpowering sense of God's presence finally came upon him. At last, the breakthrough he prayed for had come! He immediately went to the house of a friend to be alone. Moody referred to this experience as his own Mount of Transfiguration. God revealed himself and his love to him in a new way. Spiritual dryness gave way to a flood of Spirit-given refreshment. Moody later cited this experience as the moment when God gave him greater single-mindedness in evangelism than he had ever had before. From this time on he would be less hustling, less ambitious and more sensitive to the leading of the Holy Spirit. He also noticed an increase in divinely given energy in his preaching, as opposed to self-generated energy. Many others noticed these changes as well.

New opportunity for outreach

Finally, in addition to this new empowerment, the Chicago fire marked the beginning of some amazing new opportunities for Moody. It ushered in a new era of extended ministry for him.

It was in 1873 that the simple seeds for his new school in Chicago were planted. What started out as a deaconess school and a school to train Christian lay workers would blossom into the Chicago Bible Institute, later renamed the Moody Bible Institute.

In 1873, Moody accepted an invitation to preach in Britain. This would be his fourth of eight transatlantic trips in all. During this trip the unexpected happened. There was an unprecedented response to Moody's gospel message. The 1873 visit would be his first great evangelistic campaign. It lasted for two years.

When Moody returned to America, he conducted meetings on the east coast where the blessings continued to flow. So, whether it was New York, Philadelphia, Boston or Chicago, the same kind of response that he saw in Britain came to Moody's native New England and then to cities all across America. God was at work in a new way through his preaching.

Moody now became the best-known evangelist on both continents. One Anglican bishop put it this way: 'Moody took the people of Britain in one hand, and America in another, and lifted them up to the glory of God.'[22]

Conclusion

It has been said that moments of catastrophe often mark the beginning of a brand-new day. In Scripture, this was true for the prodigal son. It was also true of the Philippian gaoler. When the prison walls shook, new life came to his household. I believe this can also be said of D. L. Moody.

As tragic as the Chicago fire was, it proved to be a great turning point, not just for the city, but also for the one they used to call 'Crazy Moody'. The fire gave birth to a new freedom and concentration in his ministry, it gave birth to a new urgency and power in his preaching, and it gave birth to extraordinary opportunities. In the end, the Chicago fire proved to be the refiner's fire. In time, Moody was able to see through the smoke and recognize the other side of catastrophe.

4

D. L. MOODY:
PAYMENT ON ACCOUNT

Thomas E. Corts

These English people are the best people to preach to in all the world.

Theodore Cuyler to D. L. Moody[1]

The United States is indebted to Great Britain forever in the matter of its Christian faith. England planted the Episcopal, Methodist, and Baptist churches, the Young Men's Christian Association, and the Salvation Army, in the new world. Scotland gave the states Presbyterianism. Ireland contributed a number of sturdy evangelists. On top of all this, and at a later date, Britain threw in the Boy Scouts, for good measure.[2]

Not until 1873 was the United States able to pay something on account ... Britain's priceless gift of Wesley and Whitefield more than a century before, had been returned in the persons of D. L. Moody and Ira D. Sankey, the one a shoe salesman and the other a bank clerk.[3]

The reconciliation of such accounts may be impossible, but it is pure irony that the story of American evangelist D. L. Moody is so heavily reliant upon Great Britain. The English, Scots and Irish taught him the Bible, impressed upon him the meaning of the Spirit-filled life and responded to him in massive numbers, forgiving his grammatical shortcomings, his occasional abruptness. Moody, of humble origin and utterly without rank or obvious distinction, never met a stranger, even in class-conscious Britain, and was unintimidated meeting new faces. He pursued new relationships and was always open to new friendships. How did the Chicago mission-worker from a dirt-poor childhood in rural Massachusetts develop serious Anglophilia? He had never travelled abroad, was not a voracious reader, did not enjoy cultural ephemera and seemed little aware of persons of rank and reputation. What motivated the former shoe salesman to explore the British Isles and later 'set a torch to Scotland',[4] as well as Ireland and England?

Initially, it was the health of his dear wife, Emma Revell Moody, that caused the evangelist to surprise friends in February 1867, announcing an impending departure for Britain. Better educated than her husband and from a family of greater means and refinement, Mrs Moody was ever steadying ballast to her husband. In the early winter of 1866/67, troubled by asthma, her doctor recommended a sea voyage.[5] Obeying the physician's counsel, Moody hoped at the same time to meet special people in England, among them George Müller who, by sheer faith, operated an orphanage of 1500 in Bristol, never asking for money, but 'praying in' the resources to care for his children. Moody may have hoped also to meet George Williams, founder of the YMCA. Too, Moody had read everything he could find by Charles Haddon Spurgeon, the most famous evangelical preacher of that day.[6] Three years older, Spurgeon, like Moody, was not formally educated, was stout-framed and cheerful, attracted to good stories and pithy sayings. More has been written of the Moody–Spurgeon encounters, though surprisingly little has been written of Moody's meetings with Müller and Williams. We know that during the first Moody mission to Britain, Müller felt a special impulse to follow up the work of Moody and Sankey. On his own initiative, Müller spent almost full-time trailing them, from August 1875 until July 1876, at times addressing crowds of from 2000 to 6000.[7]

We know not how Moody scraped up the funds to go abroad, although his Chicago friend, John Farwell, is a likely suspect. Moody seems rarely to have been concerned about money.[8] His basic philosophy, perhaps, may be summarized in a statement he made years later, recalling one fund-raising experience of the 1860s. 'God gave me the money that day because I needed it. And He has always given me money when I needed it. But often I have asked Him when I thought I needed it, and He has said:

"No, Moody, you shin along the best way you can. It'll do you good to be hard up awhile." "[9]

Aboard ship, bound for England that first time in 1867, no experience in Chicago or rural Massachusetts had prepared the farm boy for life at sea, and he later recalled, 'If ever there was a seasick man for fourteen days, I was that one.'[10] Whether due to sickness or the tedium of the trip, Moody announced upon arrival in England that one trip across the ocean was enough, that he did not expect ever to return.[11] Yet Moody could not have predicted how he would be affected by England, or that he would come closer to hero-worship with Spurgeon than with any royalty he ever encountered. In 1884, remembering his first visit to England in 1867, he told Spurgeon's congregation:

> The first place I came was this building. I was told that I could not get in without a ticket, but I made up my mind to get in somehow, and I succeeded. I well remember seating myself in this gallery. I remember the very seat, and I should like to take it back to America with me. As your dear Pastor walked down to the platform, my eyes just feasted upon him, and my heart's desire for years was at last accomplished. : . . . . . [Y]ou sent me back to America a better man. . . . While I was here I followed Mr Spurgeon everywhere, and when at home people asked me if I had gone to this and that cathedral, I had to say, 'No,' and confess I was ignorant of them; but I could tell them something about the meetings addressed by Mr Spurgeon.[12]

On their initial transatlantic trip, the Moodys found their way to Dublin, Edinburgh and even to France for ten days. By the time they headed home in early July 1867, Moody had done some preaching and sightseeing. He had observed English methods, and had shared some of his own. He had inspired the start-up of a noontime prayer meeting at the Aldersgate YMCA. Mrs Moody had visited her sister, living in London, whom she had not seen in 18 years, and was completely restored from her asthma.[13]

Back home in Chicago, one serendipitous influence, deriving from his first visit to England, arrived at the Moodys' doorstep, the unassuming Englishman, Henry 'Harry' Moorhouse. In Ireland, Moorhouse had told Moody he would come to America to preach for him and, while Moody sought to discourage the young man by stalling, Moorhouse was not to be

denied. In 1868, having mailed Moody notice that he was in
the US and on his way to Chicago, Moorhouse was put off no
longer. Moody had to be away a couple of days, so he assented
to letting the young man speak in his absence. Returning, he
inquired of Mrs Moody how the young preacher had done, and
Mrs Moody told of the Englishman's impact and predicted
that Moody would like him, too. Moorhouse preached his
much-remembered seven straight nights from the text of
John 3.16 with such power as to leave D. L. Moody deeply
changed, with a fresh consciousness of the *love* of God. Later,
Moody remembered Moorhouse going 'from Genesis to
Revelation to show that it was love, love, love, that brought
Christ from heaven, that made Him step from the throne to lift
up this poor fallen world'.[14] Moody was turning a page in his
life, after having felt snarled in committee work, distracted
from evangelizing and, some say, wrestling with his calling,
whether as YMCA-youth-Sunday school worker or straight-out
evangelist.[15]

The great fire of October 1871 wasted much of Chicago,
devastating Moody's new personal residence friends had provided, as well as beautiful, new Farwell Hall, the world's first
free-standing YMCA building, and their mission church. Over
the months after his first visit to Britain, and following the fire,
Moody had agonizingly come to a gradual but intense spiritual
experience, as he spent time away from home in New York and
other cities raising funds for the new building.

While Chicago was rebuilding, and with his hastily constructed tabernacle mission operating effectively, perhaps 'desir-
ing to learn more of the Bible from English Bible students',[16]
Moody bade farewell to Emma in June of 1872 to sail again for
Britain, this time by himself, 'just to have a few months of rest
and to study the English Christians . . . determined not to get
into work if I could help it'.[17] But almost immediately, he found
more work than he wanted. Asked by the Reverend John Lessey
at the close of a prayer meeting to fill his Congregationalist
pulpit in Arundel Square, near Pentonville Prison, North
London, the next Sunday, Moody assented. When Sunday came
and Moody spoke, the morning's services were uninspired, the
lower middle-class hearers showing little interest, a cold spirit
prevailing. At the 6:30 service that evening at the same church,

the opposite occurred: as Moody was preaching, he felt the chill gone, the atmosphere charged with the Spirit of God. People were silent and responsive to his words, the more surprising since he had not been much in prayer that day. Ending his sermon, he asked all who would like to become Christians to rise, and he would pray for them. Almost the entire congregation arose. Sensing that they must not understand, he decided to re-phrase his response-request, and asked: 'Now, all of you who want to become Christians just step into the inquiry room.' So many people flooded into the room that extra chairs had to be brought in. Both Moody and the minister were astounded. Still seeking assurance of their understanding, when once more Moody asked those that truly wanted to become Christians to rise, the entire audience stood up. So surprised at the response beyond expectation, not knowing what to do, but seeking to sift out those only casually interested, he urged all who were genuinely interested to meet the pastor there the following night. The next day, Moody went off to Dublin, but by Tuesday morning he was reading Lessey's telegraphed plea to return to London at once, that there had been even more inquirers on Monday night than Sunday! Back Moody went to Arundel Square for ten days of meetings and results he could only have imagined: 400 were added to the church.[18]

Surprised, Moody, suspecting that earnest prayer must be at the heart of such a bountiful harvest, learned later of two sisters in that church, one, Marianne Adlard, who was ill and confined to bed. Day and night, prayers ascended from her invalid bed asking God to revive her church. She had read in the newspaper about some meetings Mr Moody had in America and, though she did not know him, she had begun to pray that God would send him to her church. When her sister had returned from morning services to tell her Moody had preached that morning, Marianne cried, 'I know what that means. God has heard my prayers!'[19] Moody was deeply impressed by that experience.[20]

On that same second visit, another significant event came about through Douglas Russell, the English evangelist, who had met Moody in New York earlier that year[21] and whom Moody had intriguingly heard discussing the filling of the Holy Spirit. Russell took time with Moody almost from his arrival in Britain (June 1872).[22] The two had gone to Dublin in July to join in a 'Believers' Meeting', and had spent a day discussing dispensationalism, a new topic to Moody but to some 'the key to God's plan in the Scriptures'. That evening, along with about twenty other evangelists, they had repaired to a hayloft at Willow Park, the commodious estate of Henry Bewley, for all-night prayer, seeking 'an increase in power from God'.[23] Except for prayers, only one sentence was uttered that night and it was by Henry Varley, the Australian butcher-become-preacher, who challenged Moody with the dictum: 'The world has yet to see what God will do with a man wholly consecrated to him.'[24] With such high moments and mountain-top experiences, his preaching having met with a surprising responsiveness, Moody ended up staying three months, far more involved in work than he had intended, but he left Britain in September 1872, promising to return.[25]

Dashing the declaration made at the end of his first seasick voyage, that one such trip was enough, and fulfilling his recent promise, Moody's third visit to Britain came in June of 1873. He had told a meeting at Second Presbyterian Church in Chicago, 'I want "to dream great things for God. To get back to Great Britain and win ten thousand souls!" '[26] He had been urged to return, especially by the saintly William Pennefather, outstanding evangelical Anglican from St Jude's, Mildmay Park in London. Moody was 35 and Pennefather was 57 when the two had their one and only meeting at the Mildmay Conference in London, in 1872. Moody said of the saintly cleric: 'I well remember sitting in yonder seat looking up at this platform and seeing the beloved Mr Pennefather's face illuminated as it were with Heaven's light. I don't think I can recall a word that he said, but the whole atmosphere of the man breathed holiness. . . . I thank God that I saw and spoke with that holy man; no one could see him without the consciousness that he lived in the presence of God.'[27]

Though very ill, Pennefather was deeply impressed by Moody's sincerity. He had written to Moody explicitly telling him of the wide-open door for evangelism in London, urging him to return and promising help.[28] Another persuasive invitation had come from Cuthbert Bainbridge, of Newcastle-upon-Tyne, a wealthy Methodist believer who also promised help. Yet a similar urging had been that of Henry Bewley of

Dublin. Moody had also received a letter from a young chemist and YMCA founder-secretary in York, George Bennett, requesting that, if Moody returned to England, he speak at York.[29] Though Moody had given no specific response to Bennett, he was disappointed to find upon his arrival that Pennefather and Bainbridge had died during the interval since September 1872, and that Bewley must have forgotten. This he learned first from Harry Moorhouse, whom he had telegraphed from New York and who, when the ship reached Liverpool, came aboard to greet the Moodys, though bearing the sad news that Bainbridge and Pennefather had died in March and April, respectively.[30]

Without any advance plans, and without the assistance of established persons such as Bainbridge and Pennefather, the invitation of the young Bennett was all he had; so Moody started his 1873 meetings in York, without much fanfare. There, he had the famous encounter with F. B. Meyer,[31] and moved on to Sunderland at the request of Arthur Rees. Rees, with his elder, W. D. Longstaff, heard Sankey in a private singing audition in a back parlour of Longstaff's residence, before granting approval.[32] It was Rees who first used the expression, 'Moody would *preach* the Gospel and Sankey would *sing* the Gospel.'[33] That trail of singing went with them on to other cities, building a crescendo of success in Edinburgh, Glasgow and Newcastle, where the 'Moody and Sankey Hymn-book' originated.[34]

While in Edinburgh, surprised and overwhelmed with the response, Moody, in search of help, drew on the services of young theologues from New College of the University of Edinburgh. It was Moody's introduction to the 22-year-old Henry Drummond, destined to become one of his greatest friends. As J. Wilbur Chapman wrote, 'In his day, no one was closer to Mr Moody than Prof. Henry Drummond.'[35] It was the beginning of a blessed friendship that many found puzzling: the gentle, refined Drummond 'with his occasional subordination to and constant sympathy with a man like Moody';[36] and Moody, rambunctious, abrupt and prone even from the pulpit to utter grammatical mistakes and illiteracies – 'The Spirit done it'; 'tain't no use'; 'git right up'; 'he come to him'.[37] Over the years, Drummond became like one of the family. As William Moody wrote, 'Saturday, which Mr Moody observed as his day of rest, was usually spent with his family, and Drummond was often a welcome addition to the small circle. Mr Moody would turn continually to him in those days for advice and fellowship, and their attachment deepened into the warmest love.'[38]

In Glasgow, Moody stayed in the home of Dr Andrew Bonar, stalwart Bible teacher, member of a prominent ministerial family, ideal tutor for the eager American guest. Andrew was the younger brother of Horatius, known to all the world as a hymn-writer ('I Lay My Sins on Jesus' etc.), and John, also 'a magnificent preacher'.[39] Andrew had been the best Latin scholar to pass through a distinguished high school and took one of the highest places at the university. Robertson Nicoll knew all the greats of his day and he described Andrew as one 'of scholarly habits, familiar with the original text of Scripture. But his winning, quaint, and beautiful personality was his chief distinction.'[40]

A contemporary pastor, guest at afternoon tea with Bonar and Moody later, during the Glasgow meetings of 1882, watched fascinated for an hour-and-a-half and offered this testimony of the relationship between the two men.

> Here was a man [Andrew Bonar] considerably older than Mr Moodie [sic]; a man of varied attainments; ripe scholarship; keen and discriminating intellect; a rich and discursive fancy, and under-lying all and sanctifying all other gifts a long and deep experience of spiritual things; a life-long endeavour to walk with God; not wholly in vain; and to me it was a beautiful and very touching thing to see such a man, thus hanging on the lips of the new Evangelist, with the eager timidity of a Neophyte, to whom everything was new and everything was wonderful.[41]

No wonder Moody said Andrew Bonar was one of the two men in all of Britain who had helped him most.[42]

The Americans next returned to England, to Manchester, Sheffield, Birmingham and Liverpool, ending up with a tri-umphal series in five venues around London. London meetings were designed to meet the needs of both West and East, the titled and the commoners. Many an observer commented on the great crowds of coaches, omnibuses and carriages that sur-rounded meeting sites until 14 August 1875, when the American duo sailed for home. No preacher in history had so captivated England, Scotland and Ireland as D. L. Moody. He was only 38, but from the shores of England he had aroused the interest of his own countrymen, 'a greater marvel to us than to you', the Rev. Dr Philip Schaff of New York had commented.[43] All America seemed to be asking, 'Who is this fellow who has so impressed the British?'

Trip number four to Britain began in September 1881, in response to numerous requests, particularly the invitation of Dr Andrew Bonar, delivered to the Evangelist personally at his Northfield, Massachusetts conference. By this time Moody's name was a household word throughout the British Isles. The prejudices he dealt with on his first evangelistic effort did not materialize. He found himself mellower, a little less intense, as he again began with a month in the north of England. He then went to Edinburgh and Glasgow, later touring smaller cities of Scotland. He took a fortnight's rest in Switzerland with his family. By early 1883, he was in Ireland and other English cities. A brief trip home to Northfield in the latter part of April 1883 afforded a short respite, renewing his strength for the London campaign, carefully planned by committee to run from November 1883 to June 1884. This time the London campaign employed temporary buildings, seating over 5180 persons, plus seats on the platform and a large inquiry room. They were erected and re-erected at 11 different sites, demanding a pace so lively that Sankey felt compelled to return to America to rest even before the London meetings closed.[44]

The 1881–3 visit was notable for many special events. Visits to Cambridge and Oxford that first subjected the evangels to sceptical university students' antics and ended up victoriously impacting those two great centres of learning. In London, curiosity brought a young medical student to a chance encounter with Moody, and his life was changed; redirected to mission service, he became known to the world as Sir Wilfred Grenfell of Labrador.[45] Moody told a newspaperman at the close of the 1881–4 campaign that 'he felt the work in London had been better than in 1875: less of novelty and sensation, but more people reached and a deeper impression made'. The weekly attendance was about 75,000 for 30 weeks, making a gross total of over 2 million or, in the estimate of the *Pall Mall Gazette*, 2,200,000,[46] a record that was matched or exceeded only by the London Billy Graham crusade in the spring of 1954, when 72 consecutive nights totalled approximately 2,000,000 souls.[47]

During the visit Moody was graciously provided fine lodgings in homes of British friends. Part of the time he was with the Quintin Hogg family, off Cavendish Square, near Hogg's Polytechnic Institute, which stands today as a tribute to a Christian layman with a social conscience.[48] Whittle described Moody's accommodation in the Hogg household in his journal as 'a house built by an English Duke. The rooms are very fine with exceedingly high ceilings, with stone stairways connecting. Moody has a parlor and bedroom, a servant set apart for his use, and a carriage to take him anywhere and at any time he wishes.'[49] During his 1883–4 London campaign, he first stayed with Lord Kinnaird in fashionable Mayfair.[50] Later, in the Croydon area, Lady Ashburton, a banker's wife, provided for Moody in her nearby mansion, situated in a park of 180 acres, with servants.[51] On his Saturdays 'off', Moody often invited young people to homes of the wealthy on London's outskirts for games and fun.[52]

The very best friends Moody had in Britain would probably be the Scots, Peter and Jane Mackinnon. In the summer of 1874 he stayed in their home, and Jane Mackinnon came especially to love the Moodys' ten-year-old Emma, about the age of the Mackinnons' deceased child. Jane Mackinnon wrote of their delight in getting to know the Moodys personally. A wealthy partner in the British India shipping line, Peter once said to Henry Drummond about Moody, 'In the course of a lifelong commercial experience, I have never met a man with more business capacity and sheer executive ability than D. L. Moody.'[53] Moody said Peter Mackinnon was 'more of a father' than any man that had ever crossed his path. Jane became Mrs Moody's greatest friend on either side of the Atlantic.[54]

Moody's fifth and final visit to Great Britain came in 1891, after the Rev. John Smith and the Rev. Dr Mosey of Edinburgh were in Northfield for a Moody summer conference. At one session, the Rev. Smith stepped up with a large bundle in his hands, a tribute to Moody from 50 towns and cities of Scotland, requesting him to make another evangelistic tour of that country.[55] The petition was 150 feet long and contained 2500 signatures.

Moody soon gave indication of his plans and proceeded to Scotland in late November 1891 through the end of March 1892. Moody had given full discretion to his old friend, William Robertson of Carrubber's Close Mission, Edinburgh. Robertson realized that on his earlier tour Moody had visited 100 Scottish towns or meeting halls and he arranged for Moody to visit them all again.[56] After Scotland came six weeks in Ireland and then he faced a vigorous schedule in London, capped off with a series of meetings in Spurgeon's Tabernacle. Before leaving Britain, hampered by a pesky cold and hoarseness, Moody was persuaded by his son Will and by George C. Stebbins to see a Doctor Habershon and then to consult with a heart specialist, Sir Andrew Clark. From the doctors, Moody learned that he had a heart condition and was counselled to reduce his workload and to get increased rest.[57]

The voyage home was underway only three days when a crisis developed with the ship's engine shaft so that it could not propel and listed, drifting powerlessly out of the normal sea lanes, taking on water and destined to sink with its human cargo. All on board felt they would surely die, even allowing Moody to gather them for special prayer. After two nights the ship was rescued and towed back to a British port. Strangely, the experience seemed to have cured Moody of seasickness and he was able to enjoy his trip home.[58]

After his return from Britain in 1893, Moody continued to preach in his unique style and to hold meetings in different parts of the United States. His pace was slackened somewhat by awareness of his heart condition. He died in 1899, after being hurried home to Northfield following an attack that occurred during a preaching mission in Kansas City.

Clearly, Moody was kindly accepted by the British people. Sir George Adam Smith, in the early days of this century, declared that no published record of the 1873–5 revival movement has done full justice to it. 'The present generation do not know how large it was, and with what results upon the life of the nation.'[59] Indeed, the filling of the Royal Albert Hall in 1937, almost 38 years after his death, on the occasion of the centenary of Moody's birth, was tribute to his impact on the nation.[60]

Though a highly class-structured society in the latter 1800s, England, Ireland, Wales and Scotland all came to affirm, not unanimously, but with broad responsiveness, the Americans so extremely different from themselves. Without superimposing onto history a set of motivations presumed by the modern reader, or attempting to trace today's politically correct template upon a bygone era, it is yet fascinating to note how forward-thinking Moody was in propounding in life and ministry a Gospel on the frontiers. Consider that Moody was ahead of his time on the issues of 1. class; 2. race; 3. gender; 4. interdenominational cooperation; 5. tradition and methodologies.

CLASS

From humble origins and having wide experience dealing with the poor in Chicago, nothing in Moody's background conditioned him for confronting the British class structure, still more pronounced today than in many countries, and even more rigidly maintained in the nineteenth century. Therefore Moody carried on in Great Britain in the same manner as was his custom in the United States. That meant that his appeal was to persons of all ranks and stations; one magazine of that time noted the unusual circumstance of a 'hairdresser instructing a duke' in the inquiry room,[61] with an extra measure of concern meted to those less fortunate. This classless reaching out to all was particularly impressive to Britain's masses. That such an approach could be acceptable to the titled upper crust of society is even more remarkable. One writer reported the comments of the Reverend Newman Hall: 'In conversation with the well-known Newman Hall, he made the remark that never before had any Christian minister of the dissenting churches succeeded in getting the ear of the titled nobility of England, who, as a class, were in sympathy with the established church. "But", continued he [Newman], "your American evangelists have brought us all together, and now the most common thing is to see the highest people in the land at these meetings. Many times they are seen sitting side by side with the poorest." '[62]

In planning for the London meetings in the fall of 1883, the committee used two huge corrugated iron buildings that were portable, allowing them to be taken down, moved and reconstructed. Seating more than 5180 and providing for a platform and inquiry room, the buildings sat on 11 different neighbourhood sites around London, fitting into small terraces of middle-class houses in Islington, the working-class area of Wandsworth and the 'midst of awful poverty' of Stepney, among others. The least successful venue was the only one actually in the City, at Temple Gardens, between Fleet Street and the Embankment.[63]

Lord Shaftesbury, in a speech before the Church Pastoral Aid Society, commented upon Moody's effectiveness with different strata of society:

> A great many persons of high station have been greatly struck with that man's [Moody's] preaching, with its wonderful simplicity and power. . . . Mr Moody is making a very great impression among the great mass of the people, and even among the most cultivated classes of society.[64]

In the 1875 meetings in London, for a time Moody and Sankey faced two evangelistic services each evening, one at 7:30 in a temporary structure on Bow Common in the 'poorest part of the East End', and dashing across town by 9:00 to be at the fashionable Royal Opera House in Haymarket. Pollock quoted an eyewitness as saying, 'The scene at the Haymarket baffles description. It was literally blocked with the carriages of the aristocratic and plutocratic of the land; and the struggle for admission was perhaps more severe in the West than in the East.'[65]

On at least one occasion, Moody's pedestrian views and common origin seemed to provoke the British élite. In June of 1875, he was urged to conduct a meeting at Eton College, a special place reserved for the sons of the upper class. The matter met with some opposition, even to the point of discussion in Parliament, and his official invitation, if ever actually offered, was withdrawn. So Moody preached under a tree in a private garden, as a resolution of the problem.[66]

Yet Moody's meetings, including overflow and follow-up meetings, had their distinct audiences: special meetings for women, for men, for children, for example. One report from Edinburgh in 1873 told of a man who dashed into a service at Barclay Church, announcing that there was a large crowd gathered at Fountainbridge and no one was present to conduct devotions. Dr Horatius Bonar said he would go and immediately departed with the messenger. En route, the messenger told him he had been through the district, house by house, and believed the congregation waiting for him 'would be in great part composed of the very refuse of the neighbourhood'.[67]

One contemporary summary concluded 'in these meetings the fact was clearly seen that when the Holy Spirit works, he brings all ranks and all ages to the level of a common need, and to the fountain of living waters that flows for rich and poor'.[68] Perhaps Moody's nonchalance toward Britain's élite can be seen in one incident Pollock describes. Just before the service began one evening, Sankey burst excitedly into the backstage room, and blurted out incredulously, 'Moody, the *Princess of Wales* has just arrived!' Moody was speaking to a helper. Unmoved, he glanced up and said dispassionately, 'May she be blessed. I'll be out in a minute.' And went right on with his instructions to the helper.[69]

RACE

Throughout his life, Moody accepted persons of all races. A visitor to Chicago in the Evangelist's early days, wanting to see his work among the poor, came through the door of a shanty and was surprised to see by the light of a few candles Moody with 'a small negro boy in his arms', and Moody attempting to read him the story of The Prodigal Son. Though the visitor noted that the reader himself could not make out many of the words and had to skip them, he sought to convey the meaning. Afterward, Moody explained to the visitor that he had no education, but 'I love the Lord Jesus and I want to do something for him'.[70]

Openness to racial diversity was evident in the first graduation ceremony of Moody's Mount Hermon School in 1887, when brief addresses were given by students of differing nationalities and ethnic backgrounds. 'William Moody, who goes to Yale College, spoke for the Americans; Louis Johnson, a full-blooded Choctaw, spoke in his own language for the various Indian tribes represented in the school; Chin Loon, in full Chinese dress, spoke for his nationality, which has several representatives at Mount Hermon; Thomas N. Baker, a full-blooded Negro and a general favorite in the school, spoke for his race.'[71] In the Class of 1889, 32 nations were represented and the student officer of one dormitory was from Virginia, born a slave.[72]

When in Edinburgh, about to begin his campaign of 1874, Moody encountered the all-black Jubilee Singers of Nashville, Tennessee's Fisk University and boldly enlisted them to sing at his meetings. Fisk University had been chartered just six years. It can only be imagined that, if Sankey's organ and gospel songs were considered a radical departure from the Scottish psalter, how dramatically extreme would be African-American spirituals, of which most in Scotland had never heard. A dark-skinned individual was a fairly rare sight in Scotland of the 1870s. And even Americans had difficulty comprehending the style and purpose of such a troupe in that day, a stereotypical minstrel show being the public's almost sole reference point for an all-black performing group. (For example, a Cincinnati pastor in the 1870s gave the local newspaper a notice he wanted published in the next edition announcing the appearance of the Fisk University group, not yet named the 'Jubilee Singers'. The notice appeared in print thus: 'A band of negro minstrels will sing in the Vine Street Congregational Church this morning. They are genuine negroes and call themselves "Colored Christian Singers".'[73]) Surely the Edinburgh public, to whom Moody first introduced the Fisk students, would have been shocked to determine whether they were witnessing a minstrel show or theatre act. One writer commented upon 'the appearance of the American Jubilee Singers, Africans whose black faces were ignorantly supposed to associate them with those bands of professional masqueraders known as "Christy Minstrels" '.[74] Another contemporary account explains: 'At first, the appearance of these singers at evangelistic meetings was thought too bold a step, but when it became known that they are all living believers in the Lord Jesus Christ, the voice of disapproval was at once hushed, and their help gladly accepted.'[75]

Moody's explanation, as reported at the time, is clear.

'There were,' he said, 'about three million of that race just coming out of a state of slavery, and the Jubilee Singers were travelling through Christendom, and labouring hard to collect funds, for the purpose of lifting up their brethren from the depths of ignorance in which they lived.' The Jubilee Singers, he said, had been largely patronised since they had come from America, and he had no doubt that they had the prayers of many good people. . . . He stated that he first met them in Newcastle, when they came into one of his meetings. At that time he did not know who they were, and had never heard of them. Someone suggested to him that he should ask them to sing. He replied, 'No, I suppose they are merely public singers: I don't suppose they know anything about Christ!' But when he was informed of their true character, and the mission which had brought them to England, and after they had sung 'Steal Away to Jesus', he was forced to give them his whole sympathies.[76]

Later on that same mission, when Moody was in London in 1875, he again turned to the Jubilee Singers. As the Fisk University historian told the story, 'Within an hour of their arrival the singers were invited by Evangelist Moody to sing at his afternoon service at the Haymarket Opera House. Assuming it was their duty, the troupe temporarily turned aside from their concerts to help win souls. The company secured quarters in London and labored with Moody for a month, singing to approximately 10,000 to 12,000 people daily.'[77] At the end of the month, Moody presented each singer with an autographed Bible.

The Jubilee Singers went on to even greater popularity in Britain, singing before Queen Victoria, dining three times with Prime Minister Gladstone, and singing before many other highly placed hearers, facing great crowds who swarmed their exit and reached eagerly to shake hands.[78] While Moody may later have had trouble reconciling his sense of oughtness with racial realities in the American South, he was to take a bold stand with his own schools and in the Britain of the mid-1870s.[79]

Gender

Women's suffrage was not yet law in Britain or America when Moody visited the British Isles. Women's rights were clearly subordinate to those of men. Particularly, men-of-the-cloth did not see women in leadership capacities and, while certain ministrations of the church were open to women, there were clear limitations. Moody seems to have been early to recognize the effectiveness of women in religious roles, and the appeals that could be directed to the female sex. In his Chicago efforts, he yielded great respect to Emma Dryer, a well-educated, former state university professor, whose courage and intelligence he highly regarded and who encouraged Moody, and whom he encouraged as a Bible teacher, her work gradually leading to what became Moody Bible Institute.[80] In his first Edinburgh campaign, Moody was more aggressive on behalf of women's presence than was expected. At his noontime prayer meetings, for example, elements of controversy appeared because 'open prayer' was practised, allowing anyone who wanted to pray, to pray aloud, including women.[81]

During one of his first trips to Britain, Moody had taken note of Dr Pennefather's pioneer programme of an order of deaconesses. The American's concepts of a women's auxiliary for the YMCA and of a women's aid society seem to have been borrowed from Pennefather's effort.[82]

Moody never hesitated to put women in the spotlight. In addition to Emma Dryer, the work of Miss Cotton, a newspaper reporter whom Moody put to work and to whom he later gave leadership responsibility, is another example.[83] In her *Reminiscences*, Lady Aberdeen, who with her husband had been so close to Drummond and who were strong and thoughtful evangelicals, when visiting Northfield in 1891 commented on a 'Miss Fox, a Californian girl, who was brought into the fold when he was preaching in California two years ago, and who is now training to become one of their regular singers'.[84] Lady Aberdeen went on to describe a special service at Mount Hermon, during that same visit, at which she was the featured speaker. After Miss Fox had sung, 'Mr Moody told me [Lady Aberdeen] I had to speak, and would take no denial, and so, like other people, I did my best, and obeyed very briefly, describing the picture, "Diana or Christ". They were a splendid audience.[85]

In almost all the larger venues, Moody held special meetings for ladies and/or girls.[86] In Glasgow, in 1874, for example, a special meeting was held in Kibble Crystal Palace for the city's 12,000 warehouse girls. The capacity of 5000 girls were seated, hundreds were standing, and almost a thousand waited outside. Yet another service for young women was held the following evening.[87] During one of the missions to Ireland, Moody's daughter-in-law, Mrs William Revell Moody, approached the evangelist with a petition signed by a number of young women asking for a conference of their own, similar to the Northfield meetings for men. Moody readily assented[88] and even other women's conferences became standard during summers at Northfield.

That he considered himself forward-thinking on women's issues is evident from his response when his friend, Frances Willard, attacked what she *thought* was Moody's antiquated approach to women.[89] If he had not cared so deeply, he would have been wounded less severely.

The dream of a training school for girls Moody harboured for some time. He had been touched by the three bright Sikes girls in the Northfield area, girls he and his brother Samuel had talked about on a sunny summer drive, the last summer of Samuel's life. Samuel, with a twin sister school teacher who yearned for more education, and Dwight both thought there were too many old maids and widows in New England, rural females for whom opportunity was scarce.[90] An added pro-women's influence was the distinguished attorney, Harvard graduate Henry Durant, who had founded Wellesley College and who provided lodging for Moody during his Boston campaign of 1877. Durant, as he had demonstrated with his investment in Wellesley, had a deep commitment to the education of women. Over those long evenings, unwinding after days of services capped by hours in the inquiry room, Durant and Moody fashioned their ideas for women's education. Their talks came to fruition in Moody's first educational effort, the Northfield School, a training ground for young women, and Durant became one of the school's trustees.[91]

Interdenominational cooperation

It is well known that D. L. Moody never valued denominational partitions, while he favoured all churches. From his early days in Scotland he elicited participation from all segments, no small matter in light of the dissension that had split even the Church of Scotland. A contemporary observer wrote about the Moody meetings: 'Every evening there were around the pulpit, ministers of all denominations, from all parts of the country, while among the audience there were members of the nobility, professors from the University, and distinguished lawyers from the Parliament House.'[92] 'The clergy and dissenting ministers working together in a way which would, a few weeks previously, have been thought impossible.'[93]

Scribner's magazine stated about the Moody effort: 'It brings all the churches together upon common ground. The Presbyterian, the Baptist, the Methodist, the Episcopalian, sit on the same platform, and, together, learn that, after all, the beginning and the essence of a Christian life and character are the same in every church. They learn toleration for one another. More than this: they learn friendliness and love for one another. They light their torches at a common fire.'[94]

The evangelist's ability to keep a sectarian spirit out of his work was a constant source of amazement.[95]

It was reported that 'Messrs Moody and Sankey's principle for Gospel work is the recognition of the divine unity of the one body of Christ; and accordingly wherever they go they say, in effect, "truce to all sectarianism, that the Lord alone may be exalted: let all denominations for the time being be obliterated and forgotten, and let us bring our united Christian effort to bear upon the one great work of saving perishing souls." '[96]

Moody learned that he could insist upon the cooperation of ministers and great effort was directed to the encouragement and support of the clergy. So rigid was his rule on ministers working together that he once declined a visit to Sheffield, 'until substantial unity was secured in an invitation from the evangelical ministers of the town'.[97]

In London, at a large meeting of ministers and others just before the London campaign, on 5 February 1875, Moody had been asked if it were true that a Roman Catholic had taken the chair at a Moody meeting in Ireland. Indirectly admitting such, Moody answered that he was not responsible for the chairman, and added over the laughter that his meetings were attended by 'Jew, Greek and barbarian'.[98]

It has been noted that, in Ireland, Moody supporters had been surprised by active cooperation from Episcopalians and tacit sympathy from some Roman Catholics in Belfast, Londonderry, Dublin and other cities. The leading Catholic periodical in one city gave full information and was extremely friendly to the effort.[99]

Tradition and methodologies

Moody was a walking, thinking iconoclast, who was likely unaware of most great traditions of Christian ministry. His fresh approach came through in many different ways. His own power in the pulpit seemed to come from a businesslike approach, uncommonly calm and deliberate, devoid of rhetorical flourishes, salted with grammatical errors and peppered with mispronunciations.

His work with Sankey to utilize a type of music virtually absent from the Scottish and English churches was an innovation of great significance. The harmonium in the church was a novel idea. The use of a soloist, rather than a full choir, and the soloist's personal style and interpretation, employing pathos and emotion, always considered fair game for the speaker, suddenly became useful to the success of the entire meeting. Publication of the hymnbook in an inexpensive form put hymns and gospel music within reach of the common folk, something not previously attempted in Britain.

Few ministers had much regard for time. A congregation was expected to accept whatever the minister provided. With Moody, time was of the essence. His impatience with long-winded prayers was well known. In his first 'convention' of workers at Newcastle-upon-Tyne in 1873, he surprised everyone by demonstrating his famous regard for time. 'Fifteen minutes were allowed for the introducer of each subject, and to other speakers, five minutes each. Mr Moody keeping time by means of a small table-bell.'[100] One of his 17 explicit rules for conducting a prayer meeting was to start and stop the meeting on time.[101]

With a marketer's instincts and a salesman's abilities, he put direct mail to work in support of his cause. 'A call to prayer' went out to all the clergy in Britain, except Roman Catholics and Unitarians.[102]

In Liverpool, Manchester and several other cities, a system of house-to-house visitation was put into effect.[103] In several instances, special tracts were printed and handed out, with the words to the Gospel song, 'Jesus of Nazareth Passeth By', printed in poetic form on one side. On the other side was a short address from Moody, based upon the Scripture, 'Behold, I stand at the door and knock.'[104]

His readiness to meet and plan with ministers was novel. Before his London meetings started, he met 2000 ministers in order to answer their questions and 'reduce prejudice' among people.[105] Clearly, Moody was not bound by preconceptions.

As one scans the many relationships established and maintained in the course of his British tour, two impressions remain firm. First, that Moody had a great, durable capacity for friendship, unfazed by station or rank or importance. Secondly, he earnestly and passionately believed in the truth of the Christian cause. It is reasonable to ask whether the results of his mission were transitory, or whether they endured.

Anecdotal evidence is abundant. There is Moody's life-changing impact on 'The Cambridge Seven', the bright, privileged university- men who formed an informal élite of all-for-Jesus mission volunteers in the 1880s. From families of the higher class, with money and status at their command, they fuelled the imagination of the nation with their commitment to ministry abroad. Their work had great consequence for Britain and the world and every one of the seven has a connection to Moody.[106] The distinguished F. B. Meyer, one of Britain's important well-published evangelical leaders through more than sixty years, has paid tribute to Moody's personal role empowering his own life and ministry.[107] The eight or ten Scots who, with Henry Drummond, informally called themselves the Gaiety Club and who were highly influential throughout Scotland, England

and the world, teaching, preaching, authoring, administering – all were strongly shaped by Moody and Sankey.[108] One special story is related by Dorsett, the chronicle of one English commoner, Thomas Champness, a simple, uneducated man unaware of his own potential. Awakened and inspired by Moody, he became a preacher of long and faithful tenure, who started a Methodist college and enjoyed a wide sphere of influence.[109]

Many consequence of Moody–Sankey meetings were more subtle. After Moody and Sankey's meetings in Glasgow in 1874, inspired Christians formed a United Evangelistic Association. Members and friends realized that 'the bodily wants of the people for whom the meetings of the association were designed should be supplied before their spiritual necessities were attended to. Accordingly, a few Christian young men resolved to give at their own expense, one or two breakfasts, without any hope of giving more.'[110] But funds came in so freely, breakfasts for the poor were still being offered a decade later. 'The Glasgow Free Breakfast Table' had been first attended by 300 of the most needy and within weeks the number steadily rose to as many as 2000 Sunday breakfasts. In 1884, a writer concluded: 'These breakfast meetings have developed into a large beneficent undertaking, and are justly regarded as holding a very prominent place among the various charities of Glasgow.'[111]

While much has been written of the Moody phenomenon in great cities such as London, Edinburgh and Glasgow, even in rural villages the enduring fallout from Moody's meetings was perceptible. One such witness is that of T. H. Darlow, the biographer of William Robertson Nicoll. In 1925, fifty years after the first Moody–Sankey meetings in Scotland, Darlow wrote of Nicoll's six months' temporary charge in 1874 of the Free Church at Rayne, an agricultural village about twenty-five miles north-west of Aberdeen.

That same year [1874] witnessed a widespread revival of religious earnestness in Scotland. It seemed as though some one set to music the tune, which had been haunting thousands of ears. The movement was intimately connected with meetings held in many towns and cities by Mr D. L. Moody, the most capable, honest, and unselfish evangelist of the last generation. . . . No modern mission preacher stirred such multitudes of men and women to begin a new life. During the six months which Nicoll spent at Rayne he found spiritual interest strangely quickened all through the countryside. The scattered population gathered eagerly to special evangelistic services, while enduring results were produced in numbers of human lives. The glow and ardour of these experiences left a permanent impress on Nicoll himself.[112]

From his first contacts in Britain, when he came to learn, no one could have foreseen the great role awaiting D. L. Moody, a role we still celebrate more than a hundred years after his death. British friends gave him a platform from which their land was transformed, and in so doing, they brought the farm boy, former shoe salesman to the attention of the English-speaking world.

5

MOODY AS A
TRANSATLANTIC EVANGELICAL

D. W. Bebbington

Dwight Lyman Moody, always known as D. L. Moody, died on 22 December 1899. His name is inseparably linked with that of his fellow-American, Ira David Sankey. Moody and Sankey are like Bryant and May matches or Marks and Spencer stores. Both were evangelists, the one a preacher, the other a singer. As an evangelist, Moody urged conversion on his hearers. It was not necessary, he taught, for people to know where or when their lives have been changed, but they did need to be converted to Christ if they were to go to heaven. Sudden conversion was the norm.[1] Moody preached from the Bible, alluding to many different passages in any single address. He was a man of one book. The evangelist's study, it was noticed, contained nothing but literature designed to help his understanding of the Bible.[2] He emphasized the doctrine of the cross, the atoning work of Christ. According to Moody's sermon on 'The Blood', one of the most celebrated, 'People say we ought to preach up Christ's life and moral character. . . .But Christ died for our sins. He didn't say we were to preach His life to save men. Christ's death is what gives us liberty.'[3] And Moody exhorted converts to be activists, seeking out others to bring to the cross. He used to quote John Wesley as saying, 'All at it, and always at it', adding 'Every Christian ought to be a worker.'[4] These were the salient features of Moody's ministry: conversion, Bible, cross and activism. They were also the hallmarks of Evangelicalism. Moody was an archetypal Evangelical.

Furthermore he was a transatlantic figure. Himself an American who seemed very much an enterprising man of the

75

new world, he visited Britain no fewer than six times, always for several months and on two occasions for years at a time. He had the greatest respect for Charles Haddon Spurgeon, the famous Baptist preacher of Victorian London, reading his sermons regularly. On his earliest trip to England, in 1867, the first place he made for was the Metropolitan Tabernacle, Spurgeon's vast church at the Elephant and Castle.[5] The American also forged strong links with other British leaders of the Evangelical movement. Moody was so prominent in the life of Britain that he has qualified, though a foreigner, for an entry in the new *Oxford Dictionary of National Biography* now under preparation. Evangelicalism in the Victorian era was very much an international phenomenon, tying together the English-speaking world. Moody was one of those whose universal celebrity bound it into a unity. Indeed, with Spurgeon, Moody was probably the most influential Evangelical of the later nineteenth century. Why was he such a significant figure? It will be helpful, in order to tease out the answer, to examine aspects of his career in turn.

The formative factors in his life must begin with his hometown of Northfield, Massachusetts. There he was born on 5 February 1837.[6] Northfield was a small township of attractive white clapboard homesteads on the Connecticut River near the state line with New Hampshire and Vermont. It lay in the heart of rural New England. This was the region to which the Puritans of the seventeenth century had travelled, though the spot that later became Northfield was then deep in Indian Territory. By the early eighteenth century it was well settled. In 1733 the town was affected by the revival at nearby Northampton, Massachusetts, under Jonathan Edwards. But by the early nineteenth century Congregationalism, the established religion of the state, had become unorthodox. By the time of Moody's birth the village church was Unitarian, though the family's connection with the church was tenuous. The young Dwight did not receive infant baptism until he was five. By then his father, a bricklayer, was dead. He was therefore brought up by his mother, born Betsey Holton, a forceful woman. Even in her eighties she insisted on doing the housework herself.[7] Her son took after her in strength of character. He left home at seventeen, moving to Boston to work in an uncle's shoe shop.

There, in the metropolis of New England, he was converted. While still in his thirties, however, he returned to settle in Northfield, buying a house in 1875 and taking up agriculture in the township. To visitors to his home he seemed in later life a shrewd, laconic New England farmer.[8] In his career as an evangelist he gave a similar impression, appealing to British audiences partly because of his Yankee yarns. His speech always betrayed his origins, allowing Cambridge undergraduates to make fun of his pronunciation of 'Daniel' as a single syllable, 'Dan'l'.[9] Here was a man thoroughly moulded by his Massachusetts background.

After only a couple of years in Boston, Moody moved on to Chicago, where the second main phase of his formation took place. The capital of the Midwest was already flourishing when the young man, not yet twenty, reached there in 1856. It was the railhead for beef supplies from the prairies to the cities of the east. Chicago was a destination for the annual northward trek by cowboys with their herds of cattle. It was a vigorous, expanding city throughout Moody's lifetime. Only a year after his arrival, in 1857, the great revival that began in New York City struck Chicago. Moody threw himself into its noon prayer meetings and was fired with enthusiasm for Sunday School work with children.[10] That effort eventually led, in 1864, to the creation of the Illinois Street Church with Moody as pastor. Home, church and other Christian agencies, however, were all destroyed in the huge Chicago fire of 1871. The experience seems to have loosened Moody's bonds with the city, for soon he set off for a long stay across the Atlantic. Yet he did not abandon his connection with Chicago later in his career. In 1887 he founded the Chicago Evangelization Society to sustain and develop the activities in which he had engaged thirty years before; and six years later he held an evangelistic campaign in the city during the Chicago World's Fair. Moody ever remained the go-ahead Chicagoan.

A third moulding factor was the Mildmay Conference in England. In 1867 Moody travelled to London to explore the Evangelical scene in Britain. With typical energy, he took the initiative in starting a London noon prayer meeting on the Chicago model. Soon, however, he was drawn into the circle of the Mildmay Conference, an annual gathering for Christian workers organized by William Pennefather, the minister of St Jude's, Mildmay Park. Its attendees, among the keenest Evangelicals of their day, heard messages on themes relating to holiness and mission. Although Mildmay was predominantly Anglican, it also included members of the Brethren (the so-called 'Plymouth Brethren') such as George Müller, the famous founder of a Bristol children's home and protagonist of living by faith. Moody became close to R. C. Morgan, a publisher of Christian literature and the most open of the open school of Brethren. Morgan's weekly periodical *The Christian* was to be crucial in publicizing Moody's later evangelistic campaigns in Britain, a copy being sent to every minister in the United Kingdom.[11]

Through these contacts Moody made the acquaintance of Henry Moorhouse, a Brethren evangelist originally from Manchester. Moorhouse travelled across the Atlantic in the reverse direction later in the same year. He was a self-confident young man, commenting in his diary on arriving in New York, 'Christians seem all dead', and immediately setting about correcting their 'erroneous doctrines'.[12] He was similarly didactic on reaching Chicago, where he instructed Moody on how to give 'Bible readings', that is, talks based on going through Scripture to discover the main passages relating to particular themes.[13] This method Moody made his own and it became his characteristic expository device. In 1872 the American was back in England, this time speaking from the platform of the Mildmay Conference. Pennefather, its organizer, was one of the two men who issued an invitation to Moody to return to lead an evangelistic mission in Britain. Moody therefore owed a major debt to the Mildmay circle. He acknowledged the conference as the model for his own annual gatherings for Christian workers begun at Northfield in 1880.

In 1873–5 Moody responded to Pennefather's invitation by coming to the British Isles to conduct an evangelistic campaign. Accompanied for the first time by Sankey, he held a series of meetings in York and the north-east of England, building up to a longer mission in Edinburgh. But the climax was in Glasgow from February to April 1874. In Scotland, the Free Church and the United Presbyterians had been deeply affected by the revival fires that spread from the United States after 1857, and so were receptive to a man whose methods had been cast in that furnace. Furthermore, the two churches had experienced a crisis in 1873: proposals for union between them were turned down in a heated controversy that threatened schism.[14] Consequently Moody and Sankey suited the moment. They were agents of revival and they offered an alternative to institutional wrangling.

They made a huge impact in Glasgow, where there were perhaps 3000 converts. A Glasgow United Evangelistic Association was begun to continue the work and a Tent Hall was erected on Glasgow Green near the city centre as its focus. Moody stayed in Glasgow with Andrew Bonar, minister of Finnieston Free Church, the brother of Horatius the hymn-writer and the biographer of the saintly Robert Murray McCheyne. Bonar's union of scholarship, zeal and devotion made a profound impression on Moody, who named a new building at Northfield Bonar Hall – and there was even a Bonar Glen.[15] Clearly Bonar was influential over Moody; so was the Glasgow experience as a whole. It showed that the evangelist was capable of stirring a large population. His first breakthrough to fame came not in the United States but in Glasgow. He returned to the city for a six months' mission in 1882 and treated it as the British equivalent of Chicago, a place where modern evangelistic methods could be implemented for imitation elsewhere. Moody was moulded by Britain as well as by America.

Moody's distinctive evangelistic style deserves analysis. In the first place it was notably urban. The modern city was the creation of the nineteenth century. By the early 1870s, nearly a quarter of the American population was urbanized and already over half the British population. Moody brought the gospel to this new world. After Glasgow in 1874 he moved on to Belfast, Dublin, Manchester, Sheffield, Birmingham and Liverpool – all great cities. The itinerary culminated in London from March to June 1875. Moody preached in four centres on a rota, the Agricultural Hall, Islington drawing an audience of 12,000 from the first evening. In all the evangelist was said to have addressed over two and a half million people in the capital. He returned to London in 1883–4, this time preaching on eleven separate sites. He was targeting the largest city in the world, devising strategies for makings its evangelization manageable. In the United States he similarly concentrated on cities, starting with Brooklyn in 1875. He divided it into sections for preaching in each area on the London model. Already in 1874 he had urged the need to train others specifically as urban evangelists.[16] It is symbolic that the collapse just before his death in 1899 occurred during a campaign in Kansas City. Before Moody's time, revivalism had been predominately rural. It was associated most with remote fishing villages and mining communities, and, in America, with the backwoods of the frontier. Although the 1857–60 revival had started to shift the balance towards an urban environment, it was Moody who did most to relate revivalism to the condition of the modern city. He developed the tradition of big meetings in major centres of population that continued down to the time of Billy Graham.

Moody also injected into revival tradition the methods of business; he was himself a shoe salesman when he moved to Chicago and a very successful one. 'He would never sit down in the store', a fellow clerk remembered, 'to chat or read the paper, as the other clerks did when there were no customers; but as soon as he had served one buyer he was on the lookout for another.' He would stand outside, looking for any merchant from the country. 'There is the spider again,' his friends would say, 'watching for a fly.'[17] Accordingly he prospered. In 1859, as a salesman on commission, he earned $5000 more than his salary.[18] He did not lose his business gifts in later life. At Northfield in the 1870s, for instance, he was considering buying land for a school. One day he spoke to a friend about his wish to obtain a plot of sixteen acres near his home, and the friend agreed that it was a good idea. Immediately Moody went to the owner, fixed the price, made out the papers and completed the purchase the same day.[19] He invested in R. C. Morgan's British publishing firm Morgan & Scott, which issued his sermons.[20] He also owned the copyright of Sankey's hymnbook, first published by Morgan & Scott in 1873 and immensely profitable. But Moody did not keep the income from the hymnbook himself, instead directing it through trustees to charities and later to the schools he founded.[21] Moody had a genius for extracting money for good causes. He was, according to his Scottish friend Henry Drummond, 'the most magnificent beggar Great Britain has ever known'.[22] He was also an excellent manager, ever looking out for people with the right skills for particular

80

jobs. The 1857–8 revival in the United States was called the 'Businessman's Revival' because so many participated. Moody maintained this ethos, bringing business acumen to revivalism.

His approach to revivals was lay rather than clerical. Moody himself was not ordained. On his first visit to London at a meeting in the Exeter Hall, the powerhouse of Evangelical enterprise, he was introduced as 'The Reverend'. He caused a flutter by saying that the chairman had made a mistake because he was not 'The Reverend' at all, but only a Sabbath school worker.[23] Moody created an unecclesiastical atmosphere in his missions, using halls, temporary iron buildings, even the Royal Opera House, Haymarket. His chief supporters were laymen such as John Wannamaker of Philadelphia. Moody bought an old railroad station there for evangelistic meetings and, when he had finished with it, Wanamaker took over the building, turning it into a hardware and fancy goods store.[24] Later in life, Moody urged the laity to take part in the debates of ministers and theologians in order to speak out against destructive biblical criticism.[25] And he wanted to train lay evangelists, what he called 'gapmen' between the clergy and the ordinary laity, 'men who will go out and do work that the educated ministers can't do: get in among the people, and identify themselves with the people'.[26]

Moody was eager, however, that not only lay*men* should be mobilized but also lay*women*. He believed that women made better missionaries. One reason was that during the day housewives were at home and so a female missionary could speak more easily to them; the other, according to Moody, was that 'the women have got more tact'.[27] It has been suggested that Moody's preaching, like Sankey's singing, catered specifically to women.[28] There was a great deal of sentiment about lost boys and weeping mothers. Certainly Moody often spoke of a domestic setting in an age when women were supposed to be tenders of the home while men were out in the public sphere. At a time of sharp gender differentiation, Moody made sure that there was a place for women as well as men in his mission plans, both as agents and as the constituency.

In the past revivalism had been most powerful when spontaneous. All the members of a small community could be ignited with concern for their souls. Now, however, in targeting large cities, using business methods and gathering lay support, Moody adopted careful organization. It was claimed by a contemporary defender of Moody's work in Scotland that there was nothing new about his methods except the singing.[29] It was true that the greatest innovation was the music. From half an hour before the start of a mission service there was congregational singing; and during the proceedings there were Sankey's plaintive solos – though Moody failed to appreciate them because he was tone-deaf. But the music was itself a sign of planning. The attractive melodies were designed to cater for the taste of the young, and so to aim for a particular market.[30] The missions were a form of commercial entertainment, the religious equivalent of the music hall that was developing rapidly at the same period.[31] There were also other features of careful planning. There was house-to-house visitation; the doors were closed at a specified time so as to ensure a punctual start; and advertisements were placed in mass-circulation dailies. Perhaps the greatest innovation was the inquiry room. At the end of an evangelistic meeting, those who were burdened about their sins were invited to stay behind – or rather those who had to go were invited to leave, allowing personal discussion between the inquirers who remained and individual counsellors. It was estimated that four-fifths of the results came from these one-to-one encounters.[32] The method was to be copied throughout the twentieth century. Moody was remarkable for adapting mass evangelism to a new age.

The evangelist's theological style, to which we should turn next, was the subject of much debate at the time. In Britain he was criticized by John Kennedy, the conservative Free Church of Scotland minister at Dingwall, and by J. K. Popham, a prominent Strict Baptist in England. Both came forward as champions of Calvinism, claiming that Moody was preaching the Arminian message that all could be saved. How valid was this criticism? It was true that he stressed human agency in securing conversions, which could appear Arminian, and his colleague Sankey was a Methodist. On the other hand, however, Moody's hero Spurgeon was a doughty defender of the Reformed tradition. The evangelist did not reject the doctrine of election, as some Calvinist critics alleged. Moody merely believed that the doctrine was not to be preached to unbelievers, only to believers.[33] He actually held certain distinctive Calvinist positions. In his *Notes from My Bible*, for example, he distinguishes between the *position* of believers, which is eternally secure, and their *condition*, which might lapse into sin.[34] The implication was that he upheld the doctrine of perseverance of the saints. Furthermore, he was attacked by Methodists as well as by Calvinists. It seems clear that he had forged an uncomplicated soteriology designed to cater for both parties. 'I don't try,' he once remarked, 'to reconcile God's sovereignty and man's free agency.'[35] He framed a generalized Evangelicalism that tried to be the highest common factor of the Calvinist and Arminian systems.

Part of the reason for the criticism mounted by Kennedy was the mildness of Moody's message. Traditional Evangelical theology had stressed God as judge; the more liberal thinkers of the day were describing God as father. Moody stood with the latter. He emphasized love as central to the gospel, perhaps under the influence of Henry Moorhouse. That does not mean that Moody held, as James Findlay's biography suggests, the moral influence theory of the atonement. Stan Gundry has shown that, on the contrary, he maintained the doctrine of penal substitution. Hell was mentioned, but not frequently, and it was never dwelt on. Rather Moody tended to speak of death as the end to be feared. He found the commentaries of Joseph Parker, the Congregational minister of the City Temple, particularly helpful.[36] Parker was an Evangelical, but strongly touched by modern influences and so mild in expression.

Moody was never trained in theology and was ill-equipped to read widely. Rather, he picked up ideas from the experts, holding brainstorming sessions to draw them out. The North-field Conferences were organized partly for his own benefit, so that he could absorb the teaching of the eminent preachers of the day.[37] He was therefore shaped by contemporary currents of opinion, not by longstanding traditions. The thinking of the period was being moulded by the dissemination of the ideas of the Romantic age, focusing not on reason, but on will and emotion. Accordingly, Moody enlarged the place of human volition in his system so that a person could will to be saved; and the emotion of sentimentalism was his stock in trade. The supremely contemporary packaging of the gospel goes a long way towards explaining Moody's impact.

One doctrine particularly attractive to the Romantic temper was that of the premillennial second advent. On this understanding the second coming would take place before the millennium of peace, plenty and gospel triumph: the return of Christ was to be expected soon. Such prophetic teaching revived during the nineteenth century. Unlike most other aspects of Romantic influence, it tended to stiffen theology and so to bolster a conservative position. Moody often preached on the second coming as imminent. He urged that his hearers should have 'the promise of the Lord's coming bright in our hearts'.[38] Association with the Brethren encouraged this conviction. He was deeply swayed by John Nelson Darby's codified version of premillennialism, dispensationalism, according to which history is divided into periods, or dispensations, in which the divine dealings with humanity are distinctive. Moody's own Northfield Congregational Church had as its minister from 1895 C. I. Scofield, whose dispensationalist notes on the Bible were to spread Darbyite views to a large portion of the Evangelical world in the twentieth century.[39] Moody himself used the term 'dispensations', but he was not a strict dispensationalist, referring to only three dispensations rather than the seven espoused by Darbyites.[40] Nevertheless his premillennialism was firm, He expected the world to end very soon and preachers of this persuasion predominated at the Northfield Conferences. The conferences formed, in fact, probably the chief agency in late nineteenth-century America for the diffusion of such views in the United States. Carried along by the current of contemporary thinking, Moody was in effect a theological innovator.

At the same time as Moody's great campaign in the British Isles of the 1870s there emerged a fresh movement within Evangelicalism centred on Keswick, the town in the Lake District where annual conventions were held from 1875. The new teaching was that believers would attain sanctification by faith. By contrast with the received Calvinist belief that holiness could be reached only by a sustained struggle to do right, Keswick held that it came by a moment-by-moment dependence on the Almighty. The message was similar to the teaching of

John Wesley that it is possible to arrive at a stage of Christian perfection on earth, but it did not follow the Wesleyan tradition in celebrating the eradication of the old sinful nature. For Keswick the old nature was still present, but was repressed. Moody stood close to Keswick. In 1871 he underwent a special experience of the Holy Spirit in which he received what he called power for service.[41] One of the two sponsors of his British campaign in 1873 was Cuthbert Bainbridge, the Methodist owner of a Newcastle department store, who upheld Wesleyan holiness doctrine.[42] Leading figures from the Keswick Convention spoke at the Northfield Conferences in the 1890s: H. W. Webb-Peploe, F. B. Meyer and Andrew Murray.[43]

Moody appeared himself on the Keswick platform in 1892. Yet he did not wholly identify with the movement, holding to the broader view taught at Mildmay, which accepted that effort might be needed for sanctification. His parting message to young converts at Liverpool in 1875 was to remember that they would always have two natures, flesh as well as spirit, to the end of their pilgrimage on earth.[44] Although that was formally a caution against the Wesleyan rather than the Keswick view, its intention was to dampen down expectations of special spiritual attainments by faith. Nevertheless Moody did insist on practical holiness, denouncing the opera, dancing and cards.[45] In a sense he was a fellow traveller of Keswick, participating in the rising tide of interest in holiness that marked many Evangelicals of the late nineteenth century. It was one of the ways in which Moody was of real theological importance. A stress on avoiding worldliness, together with a gospel neutral between Calvinism and Arminianism, a mild tone and premillennial teaching were to become the orthodoxy of conservative Evangelicalism in the earlier twentieth century. Moody, as much as any individual, was its creator.

Moody's social style is as worthy of examination as his theological style. The late nineteenth century was an era of the rise of respectability. Anyone, even among the working people, could aspire to that goal, which entailed independence and a certain dignity, but it helped if a person's status could be confirmed by the great and the wealthy. Moody's friend, the hymn writer D. W. Whittle, one remarked that the evangelist's greatest danger was his 'Ambition to lead and influence Rich

Men'.[46] Moody had to court his American business donors such as Hiram Camp, president of the New Haven Clock Company, who gave a munificent $25,000 for the purchase of land near Northfield.[47] On the other side of the Atlantic there were similar patrons such as Quintin Hogg, a West Indies sugar merchant, but in Britain there was less respect for new wealth than for old status. Moody mingled with aristocrats, especially Lord Cairns, a Conservative Lord Chancellor, and Arthur, Lord Kinnaird. He was remembered at the home of Lady Ashburton for playing 'energetic croquet'.[48] Yet Moody was by no means universally popular in the higher reaches of society. Queen Victoria commented tartly that his London mission was 'not the *sort* of religious performance that I like'.[49] In reality Moody should not be classed as a social climber. He was willing on occasion to resist his patrons. When the redoubtable Lord Shaftesbury asked him to alter the balance of his London preaching places, he refused.[50] He wanted the support of the élite for his mission, but deference was not Moody's lodestar.

The evangelist should be identified, in fact, not with the social élite but with the mass of the people. There have been a number of different interpretations of the phenomenon of Moody's revivalism. According to John Kent, it was an exercise in social control. The possessors of wealth and status were using religion as a tool to keep the lower orders submissive.[51] John Findlay's biography gives some credence to this view-point,[52] and there is certainly some evidence in its favour. In 1887, for instance, it was said that Chicago businessmen thought Moody's evangelistic training school 'the best, most direct, and most economical means of counteracting . . . rabid socialism'.[53] Nevertheless it is clear that in Britain, at least, Moody was seen as more of a threat to the social order than as its bulwark. John Coffey has shown that Moody appeared to represent the values of American democracy by contrast with the existing aristocratic social order of the United Kingdom. He was a common man, standing for popular principles. Moody, according to Kent, made little or no impact on the working classes because they were averse to being controlled. That estimate, however, seems to be mistaken, Although Moody disliked counting converts, it appears that he did reach the working people. At Liverpool, for example, a report of his mission was explicit that 'Rough, ill-clad working men were there.'[54] Other contemporary accounts confirm this observation. Working people were attracted, if only by the music-hall atmosphere of the rallies.

The social significance of Moody emerges most clearly from an episode when he proposed to hold a special meeting for the boys of Eton College, the most prestigious of the public schools of England. There was a horrified reaction from spokesmen of the upper classes, a debate took place on the subject in the House of Lords; and the event was transferred from a large tent to a private garden.[55] *The Times* opined that a revivalist service at Eton would be 'something to boast of in the lower ranks of the religious world'.[56] Moody stood not with the aristocracy against the poor but with the masses against the élite. He was an unashamed populist.

Moody showed a corresponding concern for the welfare of the people. His missions gave rise to major efforts in philanthropy. The Glasgow Tent Hall became famous for its free Sunday morning breakfasts for down-and-outs and its free Sunday dinners for destitute children. There were also refuges for homeless children and an orphanage by the sea at Saltcoats. A group of men associated with the Glasgow campaign threw themselves into politics to achieve Christian objectives.[57] While very much Evangelicals, they were expressing an early version of the social gospel. The chief cause taken up was temperance. Moody himself was a total abstainer from strong drink. At Edinburgh in 1874, when asked about the problem of intemperance, he gave a dramatic reply: 'It would be a happy day for Scotland if every minister hurled the intoxicating cup from his table.'[58] Moody was the moving force behind the British Workmen's Public House Company in Liverpool, which, despite its name, was designed to set up cheap restaurants without alcohol for working people.[59]

Moody is usually represented in the secondary literature in the United States as retreating from social issues in his later years towards an exclusively conversionist policy.[60] It is true that in 1898 he declared that he was sick and tired of hearing of reform: what man needed, he insisted, was not to be patched up but to be regenerated.[61] What he was taking exception to, however, was reform as an alternative to the gospel. He never objected to reform as a partner of the gospel. Thus in 1884 he urged the improvement of the housing of the working classes in London, an issue only just coming to prominence.[62] He was prepared to criticize capitalists sharply, denouncing in 1897 the payment by American employers of 'starvation wages'.[63] There can be no doubt that in his day Moody was broadly aligned with progressive forces in favour of social reform. The evangelist wanted to help the mass of the people, not to rise above them or control them.

The impact of the man, which also calls for assessment, had several dimensions. First and foremost was his preaching. Because Moody aimed for a mass audience, his sermons were marked by simplicity. In fact his style was shaped by his early talks to children in Chicago, where he discovered his power of storytelling. In his subsequent preaching Bible stories came strikingly alive. His delivery was extempore and very rapid, the word 'Jerusalem' sounding on his lips as though it had only two syllables. There was wit and pungency in his observations. 'There is no better man in the world than a Scotchman,' he remarked (admittedly not in a sermon), 'if he is headed right, but he is very troublesome if he is headed wrong.'[64] Moody objected to what he called 'text-preaching', that is, taking a single verse and hanging an essay around it. Instead he called for expository preaching, which he believed to be rare in the United States.[65] His manner of preparation for exposition was idiosyncratic. He carried with him on his travels a series of large linen envelopes, each on a different topic. He filled them with anything relevant that he encountered, whether slips of paper, cuttings or extracts. Before an address he would bring out the appropriate envelope, look through the whole of the contents, select a few of the items, put them in order and jot down a few thoughts. Hence no two sermons were ever the same.[66] Addresses on particular themes, however, were repeated very frequently. During the years 1881 to 1899, for example, he preached on 'The New Birth' no fewer than 184 times.[67] All was undergirded by an earnest manner, since he never forgot his primary purpose of persuading his hearers to decide for Christ. His preaching therefore possessed great immediacy.

Another aspect of Moody's impact came through education. The evangelist himself had received only a basic education in the township school, where he had not been very attentive. His letters in maturity were misspelled and showed a homely disregard for grammar. Possibly as a result, Moody held learning in high esteem. In 1882 he felt honoured to be invited to conduct missions at the Universities of Cambridge and Oxford. When he was settled in Northfield in the late 1870s he began a series of major educational ventures. He started by adding an extension to his own house, with accommodation for only eight girls. It developed, in 1879, into the Northfield Seminary for Young Ladies. Two years later he established an equivalent institution for young men, the Mount Hermon School. Both were designed to produce evangelists, but alongside the more practical stream there was a classical stream and the schools sent their pupils forward to élite colleges. Other institutions were more specifically intended to train soul-winners. In 1889 Moody set up a training centre for lay missionaries, significantly in Chicago. After the evangelist's death, it became a memorial to him, taking the title Moody Bible Institute from 1910. In 1890 Moody launched an equivalent institution for women at Northfield. It taught the Bible, dressmaking, cooking, drawing, music, hygiene and health, because it was to train women who could visit and care for the poor.[68] Two years later Moody was responsible for stimulating the foundation of a similar Bible Training Institute at Glasgow. The idea had already been maturing in the mind of J. Campbell White, a Free Church chemical manufacturer, but it was Moody who stirred the Glaswegians into action, suggesting the name of the first principal.[69] The evangelist inspired a remarkable range of educational institutions. Although they were primarily intended to produce more evangelists, they showed a definite respect for education in its own right. Through these agencies, furthermore, Moody exerted an influence over thousands in his own day and in subsequent generations.

The impact of the evangelist was particularly felt in the field of Christian unity. Moody was an irenic character who was notably friendly to people of other persuasions, even Roman Catholics. This quality was particularly useful on his missions to Ireland with its large Catholic presence, but it was also in evidence at home. He gave a handsome sum for the erection of a Roman Catholic Church in Northfield and in return the Catholics brought stone for the building of Moody's own church there. All his work was interdenominational. While he was a Congregationalist, his wife was a Baptist. He had been moulded by the Young Men's Christian Association, attending lectures in its Boston building in 1854 even before he was converted. In Chicago he rose to become the YMCA president from 1866 to 1870; his first London contacts were through YMCA, and he attained the United States national presidency of the organization in 1870. Its ethos was nondenominational, believing in aggressive work among the young without any restraint by particular church bodies. It appealed to Moody, who once dismissed 'the miserable sectarian spirit'.[70] Cooperation between Christians of different traditions was essential for Moody's mission, but the sense of unity that he fostered had longer-lasting effects. At the Northfield Conference of 1886, young attendees fired with zeal started the Student Volunteer Missionary Union, which led on in Britain to the Student Christian Movement. With other similar ventures in interdenominational cooperation, the SCM formed the institutional base for the ecumenical movement that was to prove so significant in the twentieth century.

Moody's concern with unity, furthermore, was also important within the Evangelical movement. He tried to keep together the diverging theological wings of Evangelicalism of his day, the conservative and the liberal. He himself belonged to the conservative strand, his prophetic view locating him firmly there. He deplored the biblical criticism that by the 1890s was dampening the message of young ministers. Yet equally he regretted the 'bad temper and personal recriminations' of some of those who denounced biblical criticism publicly and unsparingly.[71] He defended his Scottish friend Henry Drummond when others wanted him excluded from Northfield for inadequate theological views. Moody tried to bring the two sides together, aiming for a combination of doctrinal orthodoxy and Christian charity. He was actively reining in the polarizing tendency that was to lead to the Fundamentalist/Modernist controversies that tore apart American Protestantism after the First World War. Part of his influence was as a force for unity.

The personality of the man was of the essence of his impact. Moody looked a powerful character: stout, square-shouldered, sporting a long, black beard. He had a tendency to be out-spoken, sometimes causing offence, but his wife Emma, whom he married in 1862, restrained him. She travelled as her husband's secretary, exuding calmness and self-control, but she did not quench his youthful high spirits. He loved practical jokes. He would, for example, meet fresh visitors to Northfield at the station driving a horse and buggy, and because he did not reveal his identity they would assume that he was merely a servant.[72] 'You will find', Henry Drummond used to say, 'a great deal of the boy in Moody.'[73] Yet he accumulated stores of sound experience. His recommendation that prayer meeting rooms should have plenty of fresh air so that people did not fall asleep is a good instance of the practical common sense for which he was noted.[74]

Despite his fame, Moody retained an uncontrived humility. He concluded a private communion service in London in 1874, for example, with a prayer that he should himself be kept from falling.[75] Out of aversion to the development of any personality cult, he tried to avoid having his photograph displayed. In 1897 the American *Ladies Home Journal* had to whiten the hair of an old photograph of the evangelist because he refused to permit the publication of a recent picture.[76] The genuine lowliness helps to explain the verdict of Drummond on Moody: 'the biggest human he ever met'.[77] Much of the impact of Moody derived from the complementing of his sustained dynamism by thoroughly attractive traits of character.

What did Moody bequeath to the twentieth century? There was a modern evangelistic style adapted to urban society. It was not just that Moody held missions in cities, he also inspired and trained others for urban evangelism. The founder of the Church Army that often gave edge to the witness of the Church of England in the twentieth century, Wilson Carlile, first came to prominence in Christian work during Moody's London campaign of 1875.[78] Again, Moody's theological style estab-lished the norms of conservative Evangelical orthodoxy in the twentieth century. The Moody Bible Institute, dedicated to his memory, was as near the centre of the American Evangelical world in the first half of the twentieth century as any organiza-tion. Moody's views also spread far and wide through his writings, his lieutenants and his other institutions. And his social style encouraged and appealed to the mass of the people. One of the converts from his Glasgow mission of 1874, James Mathers, eventually emigrated to Australia in 1897, becoming a city missionary in Sydney. In 1901 a Mrs Jones, a woman in the most deprived district of the city, broke Mathers's jaw with a bottle in a drunken outburst. Two years later, however, to Mathers's great surprise, Mrs Jones and her husband were converted.[79] There is a cameo of the long-term results of Moody's achievement. That this set of events took place in the southern hemisphere illustrates the pervasive influence of the evangelist. Moody made a great impact on his own day through preaching, education, a concern for unity and sheer personality, but he also did as much as any man to shape the transatlantic international Evangelical movement of the twentieth century. His brand of Evangelicalism would spread over the whole globe in the century that was just dawning at Moody's death.

6

D. L. MOODY AND REVIVALISM

Lewis A. Drummond

INTRODUCTION

At times the question is asked in evangelical circles, 'What constitutes real revival and how does it relate to so-called "revivalism" – if it does?' Iain H. Murray, for example, in his book, *Revival and Revivalism*, draws a sharp distinction between 'revival' and 'revivalism'. He tells us there is an 'all-important distinction between religious excitements, deliberately organized to secure converts (revivalism), and the phenomenon of authentic spiritual awakening which is the work of the living God (revival)'.[1] Murray sees revival in the sense of a surprising, sovereign movement of God to quicken the church and make it vibrantly alive while many outside the Kingdom of God are magnetically drawn to Christ as converts multiply. He seems to stand somewhat negatively toward revivalism when, as he understands it, human structures and planned instrumentality – such as that espoused in the middle of the nineteenth century by the so-called 'new measures' of Charles G. Finney – come to the fore and people mistakenly call it 'revival'. These new measures that Finney initiated generated evangelistic efforts through scheduling dates for meetings, advertising such events, urging churches to cooperate together for services designed to reach the unbeliever; in a word *revivalism*. It must be granted that Iain Murray is correct when he states that the terms 'revival' and 'revivalism' have become confused in the thinking of some people. This confusion has developed into often using the two terms interchangeably, at least so argues Murray. The consequences are, again in his words, 'These modern writers on revival endorsed the erroneous idea that revivalism constituted no real departure from the revival traditions which had formerly existed in all the Protestant denominations.'[2]

Revivalism and its acceptance

While Murray's argument may possess a genuine element of truth, most evangelicals would see him as too critical of revivalism *per se*. To draw a hard line of demarcation between historic revivals and evangelical revivalism as espoused by evangelists like Charles Finney, D. L. Moody, Billy Sunday and Billy Graham is perhaps not wise when we consider the overall advance of God's Kingdom. Historic revivals obviously result in great evangelism, often on an unprecedented scale. At the same time, however, evangelism from the perspective of what Murray understands as 'revivalism' also genuinely reaches many for Christ and often precipitates a touch of real revival in a church, a community or over a large area. This has been seen from time to time in the ministry of evangelist Billy Graham, whose work stands as a classic example of what Murray calls revivalism ministry. What happened in Los Angeles in 1949 under the 'Canvas Cathedral', and then immediately on its heels that profound movement of the Spirit of God in the New England area, has to be understood as at least a spark of true spiritual awakening, and that on a quite significant level. While we may distinguish between revival and revivalism, there need not be a disparaging of either one, because it does seem evident from history that God has brought many people to faith in Christ through both aspects of evangelization. Although there is always the danger that revivalism can degenerate into what Stephen Olford calls 'evangelical humanism', much can be said positively for evangelism in the sense Iain Murray and others call 'revivalism'.

A significant case in point emerges in the far-reaching ministry of D. L. Moody. He was an evangelist, a revivalist if you will, in the sense of conducting evangelistic campaigns of Murray and those who share his views. Are Murray and his followers correct in their judgements? An examination of Moody and his revivalism stands in order.

THE BACKGROUND OF MOODY'S
MINISTRY OF REVIVALISM

Although Charles G. Finney no doubt personified and popularized revivalism, the methodology was soon picked up by others, and particularly by Dwight Lyman Moody. Hard on the heels of Finney, Moody embraced the principle of 'new measures' and commenced a ministry of evangelism that impacted not only the United States, but Britain as well. It was said of him that he put one foot in America, one foot in the British Isles and shook the western hemisphere for Christ. That may be something of an exaggeration, but it surely appears evident he did exercise a most significant ministry and, beyond doubt, many came to a genuine living faith in the Lord Jesus Christ through his work. How did it all begin – and can Moody be justified in his efforts?

Although Moody followed Charles Finney's lead in many practical respects, it must be said that theologically he was somewhat different. Finney, when he preached in Manchester, England in 1860, was condemned by a contemporary for his theological, Arminian stance. The charge of humanism was laid at his feet. Finney left a rather negative impression of revivalists as a result, at least in Britain. Moody, on the other hand, had no pretensions about being an acute theologian or a profound Bible scholar. He was a common, down-to-earth man and preacher. Actually, he was never ordained. He had a simple background as a Sunday School worker and his lack of theological sophistication held him in a good stead with the common people. He was received amazingly well in Britain in 1872–5. His enthusiastic reception by the average British citizen proved quite fresh and innovative to the European scene. It was said of him in the *Princeton Theological Review*, 'Mr Moody, of course, was the first of lay evangelists of this period – first in time, character and influence. And the whole Protestant church on both sides of the Atlantic believed in him.'[3] But what were the revivalistic methods that Moody used so effectively to create such a positive reaction on the part of the British – and of course in America as well? They can be briefly described in the following manner.

Moody's methodologies

It must be first emphasized, as implied, that D. L. Moody was a common man's communicator. Charles Haddon Spurgeon – whom Moody greatly admired – referred to Britain in the nineteenth century as the 'golden headed cane era' of preaching. Very formal preaching characterized the British pulpit. Moody was the antithesis of such an approach, as was Spurgeon, and 'the common people heard him gladly' – both in Britain and America.

Moreover, Moody got on the common peoples' practical agenda. He planned and scheduled what became generally known as organized 'revival meetings'; hence, the confusion of terminology in the thinking of some. As an example, on 14 September 1875, Moody called together two representatives from four major American cities – Chicago, Philadelphia, New York City and Brooklyn – to decide where he should begin to schedule his American campaigns. The conference was held at Northfield, Massachusetts, Moody's hometown. There they developed criteria for selecting cities to hold such meetings. The criteria served as something of the pattern or ground rules to determine whether or not they would enter a specific community and conduct a revivalistic campaign. Two conditions surfaced as of prime importance: first, there must be a commitment of united support from the evangelical denominations of the city. Second, a guarantee must be secured that adequate physical facilities would be provided to conduct such a campaign. These specific requirements, at least for the immediate moment, eliminated Chicago and New York City. Later in that same year, Moody laid down another requirement for considering a city as a proper venue for his revivalist meetings. He made it clear that there would be no competing activities held by any of the churches in that specific community while the campaign was being conducted. This does not mean that Moody was negative to local church programming; he just insisted that there be no interference with the evangelistic thrust of his campaign during that particular period of time. He then added one more requirement, namely, adequate financial undergirding for the campaign.

As these requirements were laid out for the choosing of venues, Moody began launching his large-scale American revival campaigns. He outlined an itinerary that would begin in Brooklyn, then move to other cities such as Philadelphia, Boston and finally New York City and Chicago as venues became available. This would keep him on the 'sawdust trail' through much of 1875–7. After that, he devised a programme of moving into smaller industrial centres in the New England area such as Springfield, Providence, Hartford and New Haven, Connecticut. In the larger cities, the effort would normally run from two to three months while in the smaller communities three to four weeks were scheduled. But the point is, Moody operated on the basis of a significant move from traditional historic revival to the new measures of revivalism. He scheduled, planned and launched meetings. An organization was put together to see that the various needs, at least as Moody conceived them, were well met and that the campaign would function effectively. It is true that some mistakes were made in this process, but by trial and error Moody and his fellow workers moved into a rather complex form of evangelistic campaigns. Out of that approach, Moody's revivalism emerged and developed. It became his pattern of evangelization for the rest of his ministry.

In the Boston and Chicago campaigns, Moody took another step forward and constructed brick buildings for the meetings. Large auditoriums surrounded by smaller offices and conference rooms were erected. In Chicago, the hall seated 8000 people while in Boston the tabernacle, as it became known, could accommodate 6000. This set a precedent, as other cities followed suit. In some cases, businessmen financed the construction and then later used them for their own businesses. As a case in point, in the Philadelphia campaign, John Wanamaker converted the tabernacle into a downtown department store. To this day, Wanamaker stands as an astute businessman, laying the foundation for the proliferation of department stores in large American cities.

Such an approach was an expensive operation at that time. Still, Moody had little problems in raising funds for his revivalistic campaigns. The evangelist had hoped never to spend more than $10,000 for operating expenses in any single campaign. But in the Philadelphia and Chicago efforts the cost rose to approximately $30,000 each and in New York City, close to $45,000. Nonetheless, Moody experienced a minimum of problems in financing his growing work. He would go to prominent businessmen and people of wealth and secure their financial commitment.

Perhaps such expenditures constitute one of the reasons why the impression is left from time to time that revivalists are more interested in money than in souls; that criticism – usually unwarranted – has arisen for years. Yet it must be said that Moody was very circumspect in his handling of these matters. No one could accuse him of seeking to 'line his own pockets'. He held high ethical standards in all his practices, procedures and programmes. He was certainly no 'Elmer Gantry' type of evangelist. At the same time, however, as one rather critical biographer has expressed it, 'the element of purely human calculation noticeably increased as Moody and his evangelical followers picked a precise time and place for revival to begin, and then worked diligently to build public interest to a high point of enthusiasm just as the evangelist and his singing partner began their work officially. Here was perhaps the clearest evidence of men seeking to "work up" rather than "pray down" a revival, as had been the case in earlier times.'[4] This comment reflects Iain Murray's criticism of revivalism over against revival: undoubtedly, the two can become confused in practice and even merge into one another in some people's thinking. Regardless of the dangers, however, Moody strode forward and, out of these beginning measures, other tactics were soon forthcoming. For example, Moody had begun in England a programme of house-to-house visitations. He employed this methodology first in Liverpool and then again in London. He brought it to America and, in the 1876 Chicago crusade, he conducted such visitations and urged those involved to carry handbills advertising the coming campaign. Thus advertising became a significant part of his revivalism. In like manner, Moody used the local churches to create a proper commitment on the part of believers to be involved in the effort. Workers and helpers were raised up from local congregations. And there was more.

Music evangelism

Moody became one of the first evangelists to use music in a 'professional' sense. It goes without saying that Ira Sankey, his singer, was virtually as popular as Moody himself. It is interesting that J. C. Pollock wrote a biography in 1963 under the title, *Moody Without Sankey*. One could hardly think of Moody without Sankey. A cliché of the time was, 'If Moody could not preach them in, Sankey would sing them in' – into the Kingdom, that is. Ira Sankey did conduct wonderful singing, leading the congregation in enthusiastic modern hymns, and even composed some music himself. He produced his own songbook for the crusades, entitled *Gospel Hymns and Sacred Songs*. These were used in Moody's meetings and filtered down into many other settings of Christian ministries as well. This was a major step beyond Charles Finney's revivalism.

Sankey was really quite innovative. He exhibited something of a deep passion with his resonant baritone voice. Sankey would sing quite differently as he ministered in the context of a service. He once asserted, 'I never sing the second verse of a tune as I sang the first verse, nor do I sing the third as I sang the second. Why should I? The words are different, the meaning is different, and so the rendering must be different.'[5] Sankey was in reality more of a 'musical reciter' than a pure vocalist. This was part of his innovative style. Some had even said that he was kin to vaudeville performers. But it did communicate. He would sing simple tunes that were easy to learn and had catchy phraseology. He was very skilful in interacting between the choir of hundreds and the congregation of thousands. As a result, he was most impressive in his dramatic effect. Moody quite properly called his partner's efforts 'the singing Gospel'. Indeed, Moody and Sankey were an inseparable team and set a pattern for future revivalists. It can be asked today, what would Billy Sunday have been without Homer Rodeheaver, and how would Billy Graham be seen without Cliff Barrows and George Beverly Shea? Moody created a major revivalistic breakthrough in that regard.

It must also be pointed out that Moody not only utilized a song leader, he also employed church choirs. Moody was always very interested in involving the local churches as much as possible. Enlisting choirs of local churches, bringing them together to form a mass choir as the background singing for Ira Sankey proved a positive move for Moody. This set a pattern that we see to this day in the thousands that gather in the choir section of the huge stadiums in the ministry of Billy Graham.

Being vitally interested in involving as many lay people of the local churches as possible, Moody not only raised up huge choirs, he would recruit a large core of ushers as well. Furthermore, he organized special prayer meetings among the parishioners of the cooperating churches. Several months before the formal opening of any campaign, there would be special days of 'fasting and prayer'. Further, churches would be asked to have special services to prepare the minds and hearts of their members and others concerning the coming campaign. Moody himself took no active part in the more minute details of the campaign, but he was very careful to be certain that every prerequisite for such an event had met his standards. He even enlisted the pastors to preach on topics which they felt were communicative to the coming revivalistic effort.

Decision making

A most important aspect of Moody's evangelism centred in the invitation to come to the 'inquiry room'. Much criticism is leveled against revivalism from certain circles concerning the so called 'public invitation'. In the First Great Awakening in America, beginning in 1734, and in the milieu of America's Second Great Awakening that occurred at the turn of the nineteenth century, invitations to make a public response were not generally given although it must be granted that an invitation to come to the 'mourners' bench' did arise, especially in the latter part of America's Second Great Awakening. But historically, the public invitation or the inquirers' meeting had been largely an unprecedented event in the context of revival. But now with revivalism on the scene, Moody used this method to the hilt, taking his lead from Finney for inquirers to come to the mourners' bench. What Moody actually did in this context was to call inquirers to come forward to be counselled in an 'inquiry room' so as to be aided in their understanding of the Gospel. The purpose centred on the goal that decisions might be genuine and real, at least as far as one could tell. Thus he popularized the 'inquiry room' significantly across the American evangelical scene. This procedure, or something closely akin to it, became standard for revivalism in America, and in much of the evangelical world beyond as well. It finds its most complete and detailed manifestation in the ministry of Billy Graham, although Graham, unlike Moody, does not use an actual room. But the point is that each 'inquirer' is thoroughly counselled to help ensure their 'decision' is genuine.

Moody, with his song leader, Ira Sankey, would usually arrive a day or two before the first service of the campaign was scheduled. They would check the facilities and structures of the various preparation details to see that all was in order. Moody in no sense saw himself in competition with or critical of local churches. He merely wanted to be sure that the programme structures were well in place and ready to function effectively. Being sensitive to the cooperating congregations, Moody's services were always held at an hour in the evening and on Sundays to avoid any conflict with regular scheduled services in the local churches. Thus he had the general approval of most pastors, many of whom assisted in the inquiry room.

THE VENUE ITSELF

As the services of the revivalistic campaign began, there was usually a large platform in the front of the auditorium from which Moody would preach. It was large enough to hold a number of community dignitaries. Special invitations would be issued by the planning committee that would grant a place of 'honour' on the platform for selected personalities. Moody himself would also give out platform tickets to various people as a favour for services rendered. It was always something of keen interest on the part of the average attender to see who was privileged to sit on the platform during the services.

It must be said that Moody was vitally concerned about the spiritual life and evangelistic effectiveness of the local churches that were cooperating in the crusade. Often, there would be a Christian convention held in conjunction with his campaign. In that context there would always be a simple stock question to be answered: 'How can our churches become more alive and reach more people?' Moody had a simple stock answer: 'Make the meetings interesting'. He felt that the traditional meetings of most churches needed a radical overhaul. He saw them as standing in need of moving away from the more rigid, liturgical approach and of getting down on the level of the common people. He advocated this not only in music, but in preaching as well. The churches' reception of this philosophy was generally positive. Still, negative reactions arose, depending largely on the ecclesiastical background of the churches.

In it all, Moody was seen as down-to-earth and very practical with people. Someone has said there was an 'absence of starch' in both Moody and Sankey in the way they came over. One time while conducting a campaign in Scotland, a local pastor was asked to lead in prayer. He droned on and on. Finally, Moody got up and said, 'We'll let this brother continue his prayer, but right now we are going to get on with the service.' That struck the heart and mind of a young attender and influenced him profoundly. He then and there decided to follow Moody and engaged in work with him. The young man was none other than Henry Drummond, who became Moody's dear friend and the author of the devotional classic, *The Greatest Thing in The World*.

Moody, as is well known, was not an educated man and at times it was said he 'murdered' the English language. He even would use the word 'hain't', which was his pronunciation of the unacceptable English word 'ain't'. But even at Cambridge University the sophisticated community and astute students came to hear him and many were significantly touched. There was such a ring of honesty and reality about this man that he communicated profoundly. And, quite naturally, he was thus well received in the American scene as well. But the question must be raised, were all of these methods, organization, planning and revivalistic efforts really the pattern that could receive the stamp of biblical and historic authenticity? That vital issue must be addressed.

The validity of Moody's revivalism

Murray sums up his critique of 'revivalism' in this way: 'When-ever wrong methods are popularized, on the basis of a weak or erroneous theology, the work of God is marred and confused. Dependence on men, whoever they are, or upon means, is ultimately the opposite of biblical religion. But where sound theology is weak it is quite possible for success to appear to lie in the very things which ought to have been avoided rather than approved.'[6]

The criticism of Murray clearly centres on what he sees as revivalism's lack, at times, of the realization that conversion and regeneration are solely the work of God's Holy Spirit. Murray correctly points out that during true revival times, the Spirit's conviction of sin runs very deep. In that light, Murray expresses some negativism to Moody's work. He quotes a statement that came out of an account of the historic revival in Scotland of 1859. An observer of that 1859 movement, in contrast to Moody's meetings in Glasgow in 1874 said, 'Its [Moody's] effects were great; but if I may venture on a comparison, I hardly think, in the retrospect, that it came up to the standard of 1859. I will not give this as a reason, but I state this as a fact worth considering, that conviction of sin was deeper and keener in the former work than in the latter ... the former work had a broader and stronger foundation. I have felt so at least. We were in 1859 all Simon Peters falling at Jesus' knees and crying: "Depart from me, for I am a sinful man, O Lord!" '[7]

It must be granted that during historic revivals such as America's First Great Awakening and many other such move-ments, conviction of sin and subsequent repentance did run very deep indeed. One must also acknowledge that in revivalism that may not always be the case, at least to the extent evident in times of true revival, and surely all evangelicals long for a genu-ine revival to break in on the scene with a profound quickening of the church and multiplied conversions. But it must also be recognized that revival in that sense does not occur every day. The church goes through periods of relative mediocrity where it would seem God is not doing so deep a work – at least on a large scale – as during revival times. But what do the critics of revivalism want the church to do during such periods? The immediate answer given is *pray*. And rightly so! We all ought to be praying for another Great Awakening. But does this not mean that God's people – evangelists included – are just to sit back and do nothing until revival arrives?

On the contrary, the commission of our Lord (Matthew 28.18–20) demands that we be on the quest of 'souls for Christ' regardless of the spiritual state of things at the moment. Jesus's last words were, 'You shall be my witnesses' (Acts 1.8); and he sent the Holy Spirit to enable the church at all times and in all situations to fulfil this role (Acts 2.1–4). Granted, God alone sends revival in his sovereign will and grace; but he does not work in a vacuum, even in great revival periods. God always uses human instrumentality in Kingdom expansion.

It must be acknowledged that human instruments are prone to sin and corruption – even in God's work. Thus the church must always be on guard to save itself from 'evangelical humanism'. But that can happen even during true revival times as history demonstrates. True, the church does need to have a clear understanding of the difference between historic revival and revivalism, and earnestly to seek true revival rather than the sometimes sensationalist trappings of revivalist gatherings. Nonetheless, we should not forget that God uses human instruments in all evangelism. The Gospel is committed to the church; thus the people of God are to evangelize *always*, revival or not. So the issue becomes, did Moody corrupt biblical principles and slip into mere humanistic methods because revival was not flourishing?

The answer to this question seems to be basically *No*; Moody did not corrupt the principle of human instrumentality in God's work of conversion. Even Iain Murray had to say he was 'thankful for the work of Moody'.

It would appear from the brief presentation of Moody's methodology outlined in this chapter that he did nothing that could be construed as mere humanism. Of course, any method can degenerate into that syndrome, but Moody always lifted up a high standard of integrity and biblical authenticity in his work. Some evangelists and revivalists may well have failed to measure up to spiritual standards, but not Moody. And his reputation bears that out. As a single case in point, Charles H.

Spurgeon had the highest regard for D. L. Moody, and Moody for him. And Spurgeon was no humanistic preacher – his theological Calvinism is known to all. But Spurgeon never saw his Reformed theology as opposed to evangelistic fervour or to the use of legitimate methods. He actually said on one occasion he would preach standing on his head if that would help sinners find the Saviour. Spurgeon used every legitimate means to help people to Christ – and that in the context of a strong theology. And Moody can be numbered in that train; he did preach a biblical Gospel.

It would thus appear that Moody and his methodology – his revivalism if you will – was genuinely used of God. Many came to true saving faith in the Lord Jesus Christ through the evangelistic campaigns of Moody and Sankey. Moreover, there are historical evangelical precedents for such an approach, e.g. William Carey, Count Zinzendorf, Charles Finney, even back to the reformers themselves. And it is of vital importance to realize the early church itself was radically innovative. True, nothing should ever be done that contradicts Scripture or merely glorifies human efforts. We all long to see revival in our day. In the meantime, until that divine moment comes, the church must evangelize with all the wisdom and relevance at its disposal in today's world. And when revival does come, God will still use his human instruments and even then the church must be on guard against aberrations.

CONCLUSION

So, may we not draw too sharp a line between revival and biblically based revivalism when it comes to the evangelistic task of the church. We have good reasons to thank God for evangelists like D. L. Moody. He has lifted high the standard and left us a legacy that continues to this day as seen in giants like Billy Graham. The church must ever be ready to meet people where they are, and to communicate the glorious Gospel of Christ in an understandable and relevant way. That is all Moody was striving to do.

7

D. L. MOODY AND CHURCH MUSIC

Donald P. Hustad

It should not surprise us that, through the centuries, clergymen have influenced church music. Gregory the Great, bishop of Rome at the beginning of the seventh century, is often credited with establishing the Schola Cantorum, which initiated the long tradition of Gregorian chant in the Roman Church. In the sixteenth century, Martin Luther in Germany created hymns to be sung by congregations; John Calvin in Geneva engaged Clement Marot, Theodore de Bèze, and Louis Bourgeois to organize the 150 biblical psalms as sung poetry, thus creating the Genevan Psalter; and Thomas Cranmer in England appointed John Merbecke to set the new Book of Common Prayer to music. Two hundred years later, Congregationalist Isaac Watts wrote psalm paraphrases and 'hymns of human composing' to give English-speaking Christians something to sing besides strict psalms in metre.

Most of those theologians and clerics possessed remarkable gifts in poetry or in music, or both. By contrast, the nineteenth-century evangelist D. L. Moody could not be called a 'literary' person. His speech in conversation or in preaching was engaging, but always simple and direct; he never bothered to learn to spell or to punctuate, as shown in the mountain of correspondence he left. Besides, he was evidently tone-deaf, like another evangelist I know rather well.[1] His musical associate George Stebbins wrote:

> He [Moody] was one of the unfortunates who had no sense of pitch or harmony, and hence are unable to recognize one tune from another or to sing in unison or harmony. But that did not prevent him making a noise like one of the notes of the organ sounding when it ought to be silent.[2]

Moody's Puritan heritage led him to suspect oratorio and to condemn the opera outright, but that prejudice was based on hearsay, not his own understanding of those sounds. His daughter-in-law once discovered that if he asked for 'Rock of Ages' and she played 'Yankee Doodle' slowly with soulful chords, he would wipe tears from his eyes![3]

Yet I dare to say that, through his meetings in Britain and in America plus the music training offered at Moody Bible Institute in Chicago, Moody popularized the new hymn form we call 'gospel hymns' or 'gospel songs' so that it dominated evangelical singing around the world for almost a century. Even more, the solo singing of his musical associate Ira D. Sankey was one of the first appearances of a new form of personal musical communication, which combines religion with theatre. Sankey's singing successors include Homer Rodeheaver, George Beverly Shea, Steve Green, Tennessee Ernie Ford and all of today's contemporary Christian recording artists. And that tradition, for good or bad, will probably go on for ever!

Moody was well aware that his own generation judged music to be integral to his ministry. Newspaper reports talked always about 'Moody and Sankey' as if they were inseparable. In recent years, biographer John Pollock emphasized this phenomenon in the title of his book *Moody Without Sankey*.[4] But, even more, Moody was genuinely convinced that Sankey's music was a powerful communicator of the Gospel message. He could sense that congregations were emotionally caught up in the words and the music of a song like 'Hold the Fort! for I Am Coming' with its echoes from America's Civil War. And Moody sounded like a true music educator when he said: 'Audiences will forget what I say, but if they learn "Jesus, Lover of My Soul", and sing it to themselves . . . they will get the Gospel along with it.'[5]

Moody met Sankey at the YMCA international convention in Indianapolis in 1870. Sankey's account of that event reveals the evangelist's brusque, almost insensitive manner which should have 'put off' the suave, fastidious son of a bank president and state senator.

Moody was leading an early morning prayer meeting. Sankey arrived late while a delegate was indulging himself in a long, meandering prayer; so he sat near the door next to a Presbyterian pastor from his own county. The minister whispered to Sankey,

'The singing here has been abominable. I wish you would start up something when that man stops praying, if he ever does.'

Pollock writes: 'When the wind ceased, Sankey began "There is a fountain filled with blood". The congregation joined in, and the meeting thereafter moved with pace."[6] Afterwards, the minister introduced Sankey to Moody, who immediately blurted out: 'Where are you from? Are you married? What is your business?'

Sankey replied: 'Newcastle, Pennsylvania. I am married, two children. In government service: Revenue.'

Moody: 'You will have to give that up.'

Sankey: 'What for?'

Moody: 'To come to Chicago to help me in my work.'

To Sankey's protest that he could not abandon his business, Moody retorted: 'You must. I have been looking for you for the last eight years.' Six months later, Sankey agreed to a trial week with Moody, after which he resigned from the Revenue department. Even so, his commitment was not final, since he didn't move his wife Fanny to Chicago.

Pollock points out that Moody's confidence in Sankey was not shared by the other associates in Chicago. Said one: 'A comparatively obscure man, his presence amongst us was not regarded in musical circles as a great acquisition to their forces.'[7]

Sankey had never studied singing formally, and I have never read that folk thought he had a beautiful voice. The reports say that audiences could hear every word he vocalized: that's also true of my friend George Beverly Shea, but whereas Sankey had ruined his voice and virtually separated from Moody before he was 50 years old, Shea is still singing with some vocal beauty at the age of 95! The descriptions of Sankey's singing suggest also that it may have been more like recitative – a sort of cantillation or *sprechstimme* in which the music was the servant of the words, and there was no hint of operatic 'vocalizing'.

In 1873, Moody and Sankey began what turned out to be a two-year preaching and singing tour of Great Britain. Later in his autobiography Sankey told of his fears that the strict Calvinistic Scots would reject his gospel solos, since most churches allowed only unaccompanied metrical psalms in their worship. His anxiety was intensified when, on his first appearance in Scotland, he saw Horatius Bonar, the noted preacher and hymn writer, sitting on the platform near his little parlour organ. Bonar's hymns were not sung even in his own church. As Sankey wrote:

> With fear and trembling I announced the song, 'Free from the law, oh, happy condition'. Feeling that the singing might prove only an entertainment, and not a spiritual blessing, I requested the congregation to join me in a word of prayer, asking God to bless the truth about to be sung. In the prayer, my anxiety was relieved; believing and rejoicing in the glorious truth contained in the song, I sang it through to the end. At the close of Moody's address Dr Bonar turned toward me with a smile on his venerable face, and said, 'Well, Mr Sankey, you sang the gospel tonight.'[8]

From that time on, public announcements for each campaign said that 'Mr Moody will preach and Mr Sankey will sing the gospel.'

A year later, the co-evangelists were in a service at the Free Assembly Hall in Edinburgh where the topic was 'The Good Shepherd', based on Matthew 18.10–14.[9] At the close, Moody turned to his soloist song leader and asked, 'Do you have a solo appropriate for this occasion?' Suddenly Sankey remembered a poem he had read in the newspaper, while riding on the train. Taking the clipping out of his pocket, he placed it on the music rack, struck a chord and began to sing, improvising the tune line by line.

> There were ninety and nine that safely lay
>> in the shelter of the fold,
> but one was out on the hills away,
>> far off from the gates of gold—
> away on the mountains wild and bare,
>> away from the tender shepherd's care.

Sankey never explained how he had the courage to try to do such a thing in front of a large audience. In fact, he worried that he couldn't reproduce the same tune for the second stanza. But somehow, he managed and each stanza was stronger than the last until he had completed the fifth triumphant strophe:

But all through the mountains, thunder-riven,
 and up from the rocky steep,
there arose a glad cry to the gate of heaven,
 'Rejoice! I have found my sheep!'
And the angels echoed around the throne,
 'Rejoice, for the Lord brings back his own.'

So far as we know, this was Sankey's only attempt at 'instant composing'. But the story caught the fancy of the public, and 'The Ninety and Nine' became a virtual theme song of Moody–Sankey campaigns.

One must be careful in evaluating the contemporary opinions about Sankey's singing. 'Vulgar' most people called it, but we must remember that, more than a century earlier, Isaac Watts had called his own hymn language vulgar. This was singing in the language of the vulgar masses – the ordinary people. Communicating emotion was also important. Sankey himself once described his singing and its results. 'You can't do it with music alone; you've got to make them hear every word and see every picture in the text. Then you'll get that silence of death, that quiet before God.'[10] Sankey obviously saw his vocation as little different from that of Moody. That is why one woman in Edinburgh said: 'Mr Sankey sings with the conviction that souls are receiving Jesus between one note and the next. When you hear "The Ninety and Nine" being sung you know of a truth that down in this corner, up in that gallery, behind that pillar which hides the singer's face from the listener, the hand of Jesus has been finding this and that and yonder lost one, to place them in His fold.'[11]

GOSPEL SONGS

The material that accomplished that purpose we call gospel songs, sometimes 'gospel hymns' – which grew out of Sunday School music that originated some 30 years before Moody met his musical associate. In 1841, shortly after the Sunday School movement began in America, William Bradbury, in the Baptist Tabernacle of New York City, produced the first of a flood of books for Sunday schools, with a new type of song that was comparable to the earlier camp-meeting spirituals – with a catchy, easily remembered melody, simple harmony and rhythm, and always a refrain. It should not surprise us that when those Sunday School children reached adulthood, they were ready listeners for more songs with much the same musical characteristics, and texts that were theologically a bit more advanced.

The New Harvard Dictionary of Music describes 'gospel songs' fairly, it seems to me:

> Anglo-American Protestant evangelical hymns from the 1870s to the present. In revival meetings, preacher Dwight Moody (1837–99) and singer Ira Sankey (1840–1908) popularized simple, strophic melodies set homophonically to strong tonal progressions in major keys. The sentimental poetry of Fanny Crosby (1820–1915) exemplified the texts, each assembled around a biblical idea. Texts are often in the first person and concern the Christian life and the anticipated joys of heaven. Among the best-known examples is George Bernard's [sic] 'The Old Rugged Cross'. (1913)[12]

I raise just two objections to the dictionary listing: 'Bennard' is misspelled and gospel songs are not limited to 'Anglo-American'. True, words and music were written mostly by individuals in English-speaking countries. But foreign missionaries from those same countries translated their gospel songs into the languages of all the world's countries where they preached the gospel. I dare say that represents the largest printed cultural transfer in the world's history except that of the Bible itself.

Songwriters, composers and songbooks

A large number of the Moody–Sankey gospel songs – either words or music or both – came from members of Moody's entourage:

Daniel Webster Whittle was treasurer of the Elgin Watch Company until he joined Moody in 1873 and became a co-evangelist. He wrote words for songs like 'Showers of Blessing', 'Have You Any Room for Jesus', and 'Moment by Moment'.

Whittle's song leader-soloist was Philip Paul Bliss, until the musician was killed in a train wreck on his way to a meeting in Moody's Tabernacle in 1876. In my judgement, Bliss was the most gifted of all these individuals in writing both words and music, including 'Hallelujah, What a Savior', 'Wonderful Words of Life', 'Once for All', 'Whosoever Will May Come', 'The Light of the World Is Jesus', and 'I Will Sing of My Redeemer'.

James McGranahan also worked with both Whittle and Moody, was a brilliant tenor singer and a specialist in men's choirs. He wrote words for 'O, What a Savior, that He Died for Me', and 'Go Ye into All the World', and the music for 'Showers of Blessing', 'Christ Liveth in Me', and many more.

George Stebbins joined the team in 1876, and wrote music for some of the more hymnic songs, like 'I've Found a Friend', 'There Is a Green Hill Far Away', 'Have Thine Own Way, Lord', and 'Take Time to Be Holy'.

Ira Sankey himself wrote a few texts, including an adaptation of 'A Shelter in the Time of Storm'. Mostly he wrote melodies that could be harmonized with three chords, including those for 'Under His Wings', 'Trusting Jesus', 'A Shelter in the Time of Storm', and 'Hiding in Thee'.

When Sankey left England after their first two-year stay, he had already arranged to publish a little songbook entitled *Sacred Songs and Solos*. In the United States, much of the same material appeared under the title *Gospel Hymns and Sacred Songs, No. 1*. During the next twenty years, from 1875 to 1895, new editions of each book were released. The British book finally contained 1200 selections and, I understand, is still in print. The American hymnal had six editions and finally appeared as *Gospel Hymns 1 to 6 Combined*. Most of the poets and musicians named earlier assisted Sankey in the compiling and editing.

It seems that careful records were not kept of hymnbook sales in those days. One biographer said that the two books sold between 50 and 80 million copies in their first 50 years. At any rate, the royalties were huge and Moody once said, in comparing himself to the wealthy businessmen of his day, 'I have had more money to give away to the cause of Christ during the past ten years from the Hymn Book Fund than the wealthiest of them'.[13] Most of the money went to the institutions Moody founded, but some also to the YMCA. Hymnbook money built a Bible Institute building in Glasgow and missions in both Glasgow and Edinburgh, and some was given by Sankey to philanthropic causes in his hometown of Newcastle, Pennsylvania.

Even more, the success of the Sankey hymnals meant that the songs they contained were being taught to congregations throughout the entire English-speaking world and beyond. In fact, it explains why many evangelicals forgot the great hymns of Isaac Watts and Charles Wesley, singing little besides gospel songs for the next hundred years.

The Moody Bible Institute

If you have read the story of the founding of Moody Bible Institute, you may agree that it seemed that God wanted the school more than Moody did! From time to time he had expressed a desire to found an institution in Chicago where laypersons would be trained to assist in urban evangelism, as he said, to 'stand in the gap'. But action was delayed, because of his intensive schedule of evangelistic travel, plus the problems he faced in the academies already established in Northfield, Massachusetts, where he had chosen to live after returning from England in 1875. Also, certain typically impetuous remarks and actions led to serious misunderstandings with important and wealthy Chicagoans.

Classes for women and men finally were in session in 1889 under the title, 'Chicago Evangelization Society'. Shortly thereafter, when reporters asked Moody what studies would be pursued at the school, he said:

> Mainly three. First, I shall aim to have given a sufficient knowledge of the English Bible; so far as may be, a practical mastery of it. Second, I would have workers trained in everything that will give them access practically to the souls of the people, especially the neglected classes. Third, I would give a great prominence to the study of music, both vocal and instrumental. I believe that music is one of the most powerful agents for good or for evil.[14]

For Moody, 'music' meant essentially gospel music, with specific training for pastor's assistants, evangelistic singers, choir leaders, instrumentalists and teachers. In 1893, D. B. Towner, a gifted musician, composer and educator who had travelled with Moody for eight years, was engaged as director. Towner produced quality music education at a practical level even before music was a recognized discipline in colleges and universities. In fact, my Alma Mater, Northwestern University, situated ten miles north of the Moody campus, established its School of Music in 1896, and shortly after, its own Department of Church Music. Two Moody Bible Institute presidents, James M. Gray and Will Houghton, were gifted hymn writers as were many members of the Bible and music faculties and other Institute staff – William R Newell, Homer Hammontree, Harry Dixon Loes, George S. Schuler, William M. Runyan and Wendell P. Loveless. Through the years, many leading church musicians and educators have been trained at MBI: Charles Alexander, song leader for world evangelists R. A. Torrey and Wilbur Chapman, Herbert Tovey, long-time music director at Bible Institute of Los Angeles (now Biola University), composers Merrill Dunlop and John Peterson, singer Bill Pearce and, more recently, choral conductors Robert Berglund and Jack Grigsby, as well as recording composer-conductors Don Wyrtzen, Larry Mayfield and Dick Torrans.

As a boy, the first choral conducting I witnessed was by a graduate of the Institute, and the first sight singing text I used was written by D. B. Towner.

Influence on Southern Baptists

Finally, allow me to cite the history of Southern Baptists to demonstrate the influence of Moody Bible Institute on the church music of the largest Protestant denomination in the United States. Like all of evangelical America, Baptists copied the evangelistic techniques and the gospel song forms of the Moody–Sankey era. Later, before Southern Baptists offered any church music education, young Baptists found their way to Chicago to study under D. B. Towner, among them

I. E. Reynolds, who became the first director of music at Southwestern Baptist Theological Seminary, and E. O. Sellers and W. Plunkett Martin, first music teachers at the Bible institute which later became New Orleans Baptist Theological Seminary. These were the very first official teachers of church music among Southern Baptists.

In his story of Southwestern's School of Church Music, William J. Reynolds writes about his uncle Isham Reynolds:

> Preparing the course offerings for the first semester [in 1915], Reynolds remembered his experiences at Moody Bible Institute and sought the counsel of his teacher, Dr D. B. Towner. . . . Southwestern Seminary's School of Church Music was, at its beginning, a child of Moody Bible Institute, which provided the pattern upon which the school was begun.[15]

That influence continues to the present day. I. E. Reynolds' first class at Southwestern included one Benjamin Baylus McKinney, Southern Baptists' most important gospel song composer, who became the first head of their Church Music Department in 1941. Bill Reynolds doesn't mention it in the same volume, but his father, George Washington Reynolds, was also trained as an evangelistic musician at Moody. Bill too studied at Southwestern Seminary, became the third head of our Church Music Department, was editor of *Baptist Hymnal*, 1975, and for a term was president of the Hymn Society in the United States and Canada. He recently retired as 'distinguished professor of church music' at Southwestern Seminary.

Such is the influence of D. L. Moody on Church Music in America, in Britain and around the world.

8

POWER – 'IN' AND 'UPON': A MOODY SERMON

Derek Tidball

If C. S. Lewis was the 'most reluctant convert in all England'[1] D. L. Moody was probably the most surprising evangelist in all history. If C. S. Lewis came to faith because of the 'unrelenting approach of Him whom [he] so earnestly desired not to meet',[2] then, conversely, D. L. Moody brought thousands to faith because of the unrelenting empowerment of God's Spirit whom he desired to serve.

D. L Moody had many positive qualities which, superficially at least, appeared to equip him for his calling as a revivalist. He was a passionate man and he was a natural salesman. He could sell shoes prodigiously and, in like manner, he could give Jesus away phenomenally. But, for all that, he was not an ideal man for God to choose to be an extraordinary evangelist.

He came from nowhere, without natural connections and advantages. He lacked an education and was limited, at least to start with, in written and spoken English. Matthew Parris, the English political commentator, once wrote about John Prescott, currently deputy Prime Minister of the United Kingdom, who is affectionately know for his ability to murder the English language, that he 'went 12 rounds with the English language and left it slumped and bleeding over the ropes'.[3] Such words may be an overstatement when applied to D. L. Moody but they bear some passing resemblance to the truth.

During his early days he was known as 'Crazy Moody'. His enthusiasm almost certainly outran his wisdom, taking its toll, as so often, on his wife and children. We need to acknowledge honestly that Moody could, on occasions, be a man of very short temper. More than once he had to write a postcard apologizing to someone when he had caused offence either by not paying them sufficient attention or by responding to them unwisely and in haste.[4] Sometimes, natural organizer though he might have been, he would fail to follow issues through sufficiently, leaving fellow-workers unsupported and insecure in their work. He did not always give the attention to the necessary details of business, especially as his vast evangelical enterprises grew. This is seen with amusing clarity in the organization (or lack of it) of some of his most significant evangelistic tours. Some of them happened more by accident than design. Thus, although he had been urged in 1872 by William Pennefather, who believed that he 'was one for whom God had prepared a great work',[5] to return to Great Britain, expenses paid, when he did return the following year, it was without any guarantee of the necessary arrangements being in place. He arrived in Liverpool only to discover that Pennefather had died in the meantime and there was no one to meet him, let alone sponsor him. He and Sankey were, as he commented, left stranded, 'a couple of white elephants'.[6] What is more, he would often lack social graces, which could prove very uncomfortable, at least, to his audiences in English class-ridden society. He had his faults!

So let us not make a saint out of Moody. Indeed, one of his very attractive qualities is precisely his ordinariness, his humanity and his limitations. And yet, he became a remarkable evangelist who in his 1875 mission to London alone would preach to two and a half million people. Even his critics agreed that he 'reduced the population of hell by a million souls'.[7] God surprisingly transformed this humble, ordinary shoe salesman into a preacher who could proclaim the gospel persuasively to peers and paupers, to duchesses and dockers alike.[8] Why was this? How? What made the difference?

The answer is the Holy Spirit. No doubt, there were other factors involved. He had, for example, learned through the example of Harry Moorhouse, a Lancashire lad, to preach the love of God rather than to harass people into heaven through the harsh threat of hell.[9] But others knew how to do that without the same effect. D. L. Moody, however, was the one called in God's sovereign purposes to be the chosen instrument of revival in his day and to be anointed by the Holy Spirit with remarkable power.

MOODY'S EXPERIENCE

Moody's success cannot be divorced from Moody's own experience of God and, in particular, his experience of the Holy Spirit. In his early days, working for the YMCA in Chicago, he engaged in ceaseless activity. He neglected his family while he dashed breathlessly around from one place to another seeking constantly to make Christ known. Then in 1868, two women, Sarah Cooke and Mrs W. R. Hawkhurst, had a burden to pray for Mr Moody and had the courage to tell him so. Rather than welcoming it, Moody rebuked them. Why bother praying for him when they should be praying for the unsaved? They were the ones who needed prayer. But they persisted. 'No, Mr Moody, it is you we need to pray for.' He needed power – power to work in God's strength rather than simply with human energy through his own determined efforts. And so he was persuaded to join them for prayer on Friday lunchtimes. He began to cry out with increasing urgency and to pray for a baptism of fire, a baptism of the Holy Spirit (a baptism, it should be said, that did not carry the overtones of the more recent Pentecostal and charismatic movements since the phrase would have been used less precisely). He wanted a fresh infilling of the Holy Spirit on his life. His prayers got increasingly desperate.

Four months of struggle ensued during which time the great Chicago fire reduced the city to ashes. His spiritual anguish was transferred to New York where one day he was walking down one of its prominent streets when the fire of the Holy Spirit fell on him. He immediately turned into the house of a friend who instantly wanted to offer him refreshment. But he asked for a room where he could be alone. There he encountered the glory of the Lord. There he had his own experience of the transfiguration. There he fully surrendered to God. He later wrote: 'Ah, what a day! I cannot describe it, I seldom refer to it, it is almost too sacred an experience to name – Paul had an experience of which he never spoke for 14 years – I can only say God revealed himself to me and I had such an experience of his love that I had to ask him to stay his hand.'[10]

That experience became the hallmark of his subsequent ministry. Behind D. L. Moody the evangelist, the revivalist, the social activist, the reformer, the educationalist and founder of the Moody Bible Institute (as it came to be known) and the pastor of Moody Tabernacle in Illinois Street, Chicago was a man who had been deeply blessed by the Holy Spirit.

Here, then, was a man who had benefited from the prayers of others and would continue to do so. When he came to the United Kingdom he met with great success, which must be partly explained in terms of the prayer ministry of another woman. Marianne Adlard was a bedridden infirm young woman who had read of his ministry and prayed that God would send him to Britain and bring revival through him. She prayed for him daily in a room she could never leave but one that was filled with the presence of God.[11] When the outward signs of his arrival in Britain did not seem promising, prayer had prepared the path and the Holy Spirit was ready to ignite the gospel fire. Thank God for Sarah Cooke, Mrs Hawkhurst and Marianne Adlard.

Moody's theology

Given his experience, Moody inevitably began to speak of the Holy Spirit and construct a theology of the Spirit. For him, theology was simply a combination of the study of the word of God and the experience of God in his life. Consequently, the Holy Spirit assumed a significant place in his thinking. James Findlay asserts of Moody that, 'In the revivalist framework of ideas, the power and work of the Holy Spirit were of almost equal significance to that of Christ.'[12] Moody's theology is often summed up in three Rs. Men and women were: *Ruined* by the fall, *Redeemed* by the blood of Christ and *Regenerated* by the Holy Spirit. He certainly preached the cross, the blood, and Jesus. But it was not Jesus only; it was Jesus *and* the Holy Spirit. The Holy Spirit, Findlay asserts, had a vital four-fold role in relation to the gospel.[13] The Holy Spirit:

- worked regeneration in people's lives
- produced post-conversion fruit in converts' lives
- gave liberty in believers' lives *and*
- power to sustain them for and make them fruitful in service

Moody believed that every believer had the Holy Spirit 'in' them. This must be so by definition, he argued, or else they could not have believed or taken a stand for God. But, he said, 'the Holy Spirit "in" us is one thing, and the Holy Spirit "on" us is another'.[14] He took people back to Acts 1.8, 'Ye shall receive power, after that the Holy Ghost is come upon you, and you shall be witnesses unto me both in Jerusalem, and in all Judea, and in Samaria, and unto the uttermost part of the earth.'[15] He believed that there was a special endowment which brought the believer power and with it the ability to win people to Jesus Christ.

This experience was not, for him, just reserved for the Day of Pentecost. Nor was it a one-off, merely an exceptional event in the initial history of the church. He believed the Acts of the Apostles taught that this was to be the recurring experience of all believers. From Acts 1.8 he turned people to Acts 4.31.[16] There the disciples were gathering for prayer following the arrest and then release of Peter and John for healing a lame man. 'And when they had prayed, the place was shaken where they were assembled together; and they were all filled with the Holy Ghost, and they spoke the word of God with boldness.' That, he said, proved that such experiences were not confined to Pentecost but were to be entered into time and again by believers. It also highlighted the connection between a fresh visitation of the Spirit and witnessing, for it was when they were filled with the Spirit that they spoke the word of God 'boldly'. Without the Holy Spirit there would have been timidity, weakness and ineffectiveness.

To this he added the case of the believers in Ephesus, in Acts 19, who were asked whether they had received the Holy Spirit.[17] Without such a filling of the Spirit, he lamented, you could add a hundred members to the church but not add at all to its power. For power, the Holy Spirit was needed.

Moody's exhortation

On the basis of this theology he exhorts the believers of his own day, and ours, to seek not just the Holy Spirit 'in' them but also 'on' them. In his sermon, 'Power – "In" and "Upon" ' he sets out the need to the church.

Power: the greatest need
The greatest lack of the church, he claims, is a want of power. How could believers see their relatives and neighbours going to eternal ruin and not be concerned to speak to them about Christ? Something, surely, must be wrong with a church like that. Yet, from what he writes it is apparent that not all would agree with him that the problem lay in a lack of power. Many saw the source of the trouble as lying elsewhere.

> A great many people are thinking we need new measures, that we need new churches, that we need new organs, and that we need new choirs, and all these new things. That is not what the church of God needs today. It is *the old power* that the Apostles had, which we want; and if we have that in our churches, there will be new life. Then we shall have new ministers, not the same old ministers, renewed with power; filled with the Spirit.[18]

Not many people today would attribute the decline of the church in the United Kingdom to the need for new organs and choirs. Most would now argue quite the reverse. It is getting rid of the organs and the choirs that will release the church, they say, from a long-standing cultural captivity and enable it to communicate the gospel convincingly to a contemporary world. But in spite of its modern garb, underneath such a suggestion lies the very attitude that Moody here condemns. The mentality remains the same, whatever form the present outworking of it might take. In Moody's day it was, 'Let's beautify our churches, enhance the cultural quality of our worship by installing wonderful pipe organs to displace the old harmoniums and train professional choirs to produce exquisite music.' Today it is, 'Let's get rid of the organs, choirs and buildings which smack of yesteryear and let's restore popular culture, language and dress codes to the church through the use of guitars, worship bands, modern technology, contemporary songs and through pastors and priests that look like ordinary human beings.' But we still believe that the adjustment of the outward packaging of the gospel, the adoption of new methods, holds the secret to successful evangelism. The truth is, we have tried it all and it has proved to be no more successful than old-fashioned ways.[19] The answer does not appear to lie in methods, but as Moody correctly diagnosed, in a want of power. To bypass that answer is to condemn the church to yet more failure.

Europe, more than America, suffers from a religious economy that had grown weary from over a century of decline and struggle. The dramatic rise of unbelief and cynicism about spiritual issues has taken its toll. The churches have, despite a popular view to the contrary, been very up for change and have engaged in much modernizing, especially in the field of communication. They have not lacked innovation. But they have lacked the old power.

Moody pointed out that churches needed spiritual irrigation if they were to produce fruitful crops.[20] He reached back to his childhood upbringing on the family homestead in Northfield, Massachusetts (one suspects that Moody always remained a farmer at heart) for an illustration. He describes with graphic power looking at a valley and seeing one side green with crops and the other barren and fruitless. What was it that made the difference? The side that was green and fertile had been irrigated by the farmer with water. The side that was barren had received no such treatment. Our churches, he said, needed to be irrigated with the Holy Spirit. But, even more particularly, we needed to be 'artesian wells'. Other pumps demanded pumping, pumping, pumping, as he obviously well remembered. That was hard work, but unproductive. And many ministers appeared to be doing just that in their pulpits. But, oh for a continual flow of God's grace that did not depend on resorting to such methods. 'You cannot get water out of a dry well,' he proclaimed, 'there must be something in the well, or you cannot get anything out.' And that was exactly the problem with so much energetic but unanointed activity in the church.[21] All the new measures in Christendom will prove futile, if the well is dry.

Wait: the way to power

So the greatest need now, as then, is the need of power. But how is power to be obtained? Moody's answer is to wait on God until it comes. That demands we resist the temptation to activity. David Bebbington has taught us that 'activism' is one of the cardinal characteristics of the Evangelical movement.[22] Our activism arises from the best of motives. We desire to see others converted and therefore use every means and all our energy and ingenuity to that end. It results in busy lives and busy churches. Mark Noll has made a similar comment in reference to America. 'The tendency of American evangelicals, when confronted with a problem, is to act.'[23] His concern is that as a result of this tendency Evangelicals frequently fail to think, deeply, wisely or strategically. So, he wryly adds, 'For the sake of Christian thinking, that tendency must be suppressed.' Moody was equally concerned about resisting the temptation of activism, but for a different reason. Activism frequently led to fruitlessness because it was not impregnated with the Spirit's power.

What of the objection that doing something was better than sitting around and doing nothing? Is there not an urgency about the task? Are we not wasting precious time if all we do is wait? Moody confronted these criticisms head-on. 'Some people think that they are losing time if they wait on God for his power; and so they go and work, without unction; they are working without any anointing; they are working without any power.'[24] He could see no point in doing so at all. Since such activity would inevitably prove unproductive, why do it? Such people might as well wait. Moreover, if they waited they would be doing exactly what Jesus told his disciples to do when he instructed them to wait for Pentecost, even though the Holy Spirit was already 'in' them, as the Gospel accounts make clear. They had to wait until he came 'upon' them. Only then could they be effective in service. So why should it be different for us? In other words, nothing was to be lost and much to be gained by waiting.

Thirst: the desire for power

To waiting, Moody added thirsting as a precondition for the Spirit's anointing. He asked whether people really wanted the power. 'The great question before us now is, Do we want it?'[25] In

Moody's view it was the absence of any serious hunger and thirst for power that prevented the church from experiencing it. They were not committed to seeking it, even if they glibly acknowledged that it would be a good thing to have. He was convinced that if the church genuinely sought power from God they would receive it.

> We all need it together; and let us rest not day nor night until we possess it. If that is the uppermost thought in our hearts, God will give it to us; He will grant us the blessing, if we just hunger and thirst for it, and say, 'God helping me, I will not rest until endued with power from on high'.[26]

Why should people not want such power? The question remains a pertinent one for the contemporary church. It is one to which there are several answers.

First, we often prefer to do things our way rather than God's. We neither want to give up control, nor status. We are more comfortable in thinking that we should be able to organize a response to the gospel by more conventional, worldly means – like advertising, good publicity, contemporary music, academic argument, entertaining speakers and by getting celebrities to give their testimonies – than in God's way which, consistent with the cross of Christ, is through weakness.[27] That way we feel much more on a level with the world and we shake off the very thing that the early church took glory in, namely, that they were among the poor, weak, insignificant and powerless in the world. We will demonstrate our power, our cleverness and our importance. But the one thing this will not do is to demonstrate the 'knowledge of the glory of God in the face of Christ Jesus'[28] since such an approach is not compatible with his gospel. It will not display the glory of God for we cannot display his glory and our own at the same time.

Second, we often want the power but are not prepared to meet the conditions of receiving it. God will not give his power to those who tolerate sin in their lives. Arrogant impatience for power for its own sake and selfish ambition will not yield the desired result.[29]

Third, many do not thirst for God with the passion Moody commended lest God should quench their thirst, meet them powerfully in their request and change them.

Of one thing Moody was sure. God wanted to bless his people. He wanted to shine on his world, to lift up his work, to give his people power.[30] If we seek his blessing with all our hearts, we will obtain it. The blockage does not lie with God. It lies in the half-hearted desire of his people and their lack of seriousness about the work of God.

Keep filled: we leak

Is this waiting on God and thirsting for his anointing, once granted, a one-off second blessing, as some would teach? Having experienced it, does it guarantee fruitfulness from then on? Not for Moody. He was aware that we needed to keep on seeking such anointing. We need to keep fresh. The fact is, to use Moody's typically down-to-earth way of putting it, that when the Holy Spirit comes, he comes to 'leaky vessels'. We may be filled now, but we lose the Holy Spirit within and 'we have to keep right under the fountain all the time and so have a fresh supply'.[31] The supply of ten years ago will not do. Because we leak we need to seek the Holy Spirit for today. We are in constant need of fresh power, fresh supplies, fresh anointing.

The result of such anointing is that we shall preach Christ and preach him effectively. We will not be talking of self. We shall not exhibit anything of self. We shall be concerned for God and his glory alone.

We may wish to argue about the finer points of Moody's theology. We may want to express things differently than he did. We may not feel as easy about the rigid distinction between power 'in' and power 'upon' as he was. But the evidence is surely all around that what we desperately need is the power, whatever language we use, and whether 'in' or 'upon'. We need the fresh anointing of the Holy Spirit and Moody challenges us to ask for it. He challenges us as to whether we are going to wait for it, hunger and thirst for it, find it and then seek it again, or not. Without it, all our other activity will have no value.

Moody finished his exhortation by wishing that the spirit of Elijah that fell on Elisha and gave to Elisha a double portion of Elijah's God, would fall again. He urged his hearers, and us through them, to cry out until we too received a double portion of Elijah's God, confident that 'If we seek for it we shall have it'.[32]

9

MR MOODY'S LIFE TEXT

Warren W. Wiersbe

Walter Hooper said to C. S. Lewis one day, 'I saw the strangest epitaph. It said: "Here lies an atheist – all dressed up and no place to go." ' Lewis quietly replied, 'I bet he wishes that were true.'

For some reason, I've always had an interest in epitaphs and the last words of saints and sinners. Some of them preach powerful sermons. Here's one of my favourite epitaphs:

> Pause, my friend, as you go by.
> As you are now, so once was I.
> As I am now, so you will be.
> Prepare, my friend, to follow me!

I understand that somebody attached a note to this epitaph that read:

> To follow you is not my intent,
> Until I know which way you went.

I told my wife that my epitaph should read, 'He has met his last deadline.'

Mr Moody was a great fundraiser, and he jokingly suggested that his epitaph should be from Luke 16.22, 'And it came to pass that the beggar died' (King James Version). Five years before he died, Mr Moody had a second suggestion, this time from Mark 14.8, where Jesus said of Mary and her gift, 'She hath done what she could' (King James Version). 'Just put on my gravestone,' said Moody, " 'He has done what he could." '

One rainy day, my wife and I drove into Northfield, Massachusetts, to visit Mr Moody's grave. We walked up to Round Top, where Mr and Mrs Moody are buried, and there we read his epitaph, taken from the Authorized [King James] Version of 1 John 2.17, 'He that doeth the will of God abideth forever.' That's a great verse to ponder at the dawn of a new millennium. The New International Version translates it, 'The man who does the will of God lives forever.' Whether he admitted it or not, this was Mr Moody's life verse. Not only is it inscribed on his gravestone, but a framed copy hung over the mantle in his private room at the Bible Institute in Chicago.

As I have pondered this statement, it has reminded me that, like D. L. Moody, *we must live for something essential – the will of God*. The will of God isn't something optional, like a CD player in a car. The will of God is something essential, like the motor and the steering wheel in a car. God's will isn't a luxury for a spiritual élite; it's a necessity for all of God's people.

It is tragic when people get the idea that the will of God is punishment. Quite the contrary is true: the will of God is nourishment. Jesus said, 'My food is to do the will of him who sent me and to finish his work' (John 4.34). God's will for us is the expression of God's love for us. 'But the plans of the Lord stand firm forever, the purposes of his heart through all generations' (Ps. 33.11). The will of God is the proof of the love of God and it comes from his heart. That is why God's will to the obedient believer is always 'good, pleasing and perfect' (Rom. 12.2).

Early in his Christian life, Mr Moody did not have an easy time determining the will of God. He arrived in Chicago on 18 September 1856 and began selling shoes for Wiswall's on Lake Street. He also started getting involved in Sunday School work and, by June 1860, he had left the shoe business and was very busy in full-time Christian work. He conducted a large Sunday School and started a church and was busy with the YMCA. He was an active man, always ready for the next challenge, but something was missing in his life. For the next twelve years, he was looking for that one thing God had called him to do.

In June 1871, two somewhat eccentric but devoted Christian women told Mr Moody that they were praying for him, and he told them to pray for the lost sinners! But soon, Aunt Sarah Cooke and Mrs Hawkhurst were praying with Mr Moody every Friday, and Moody was dead in earnest to receive God's power for his busy ministry. Moody lost everything in the Chicago fire in October, and then went to New York City to preach and to raise funds for his Chicago ministries. It was while he was walking down Wall Street that he experienced a gracious enduement of the Spirit's power and his ministry was never the same again.

The next year, Mr Moody went to Great Britain. While chatting with friends in Dublin, he heard Henry Varley say, 'The world has yet to see what God will do with and for and through and in and by the man who is fully and wholly consecrated to Him.' Mr Moody's response was to determine in his heart, with God's help, to be that man. It was then that he began to concentrate on evangelism, which was the will of God for his life. The next year, Moody and Sankey returned to Great Britain and had one triumphant campaign after another from June 1873 to August 1875, and thousands were brought into the family of God. Moody was discovered in Great Britain and then returned home to be discovered in the United States.

It took twelve years for Mr Moody to focus on the one thing God had called him to do, but once he had found his calling, he never turned back. He was a man born in poverty, not very well educated, lacking Christian training and even lacking ordination; and yet he gave all that he had to doing the will of God. The will of God is something essential, and it was the making of D. L. Moody's life and ministry.

Mr Moody not only lived for something essential, but *he did something exceptional – he obeyed the will of God.*

It is good for us to discuss the will of God, read books about the will of God, and even preach about the will of God; but the important thing is that we *do* the will of God. Mr Moody did the will of God in spite of ridicule and opposition. Some of the people in Chicago called him 'Crazy Moody'. Well, he was in good company, because people said that Paul and Jesus were crazy. In his personal work, he did not hesitate to confront total strangers with the Gospel. One day he had been studying the grace of God in the Bible, and he became so overwhelmed with the subject that he left the house and asked the first man he met, 'What do you know about grace?' The startled man replied, 'Grace who?' And Moody told him about the grace of God.

To use current terminology, most of us like to 'go with the flow'. It is not that we are excessively sinful, but we just do what other Christians do. Then along comes a man like D. L. Moody who dared to obey the will of God, who dared to be different; and look what the Lord accomplished! When Moody preached at Cambridge University, the students came to laugh and remained to pray. This happened in city after city.

When he ministered here on earth, Jesus had problems with disciples who did not do the will of God. 'Why do you call me "Lord, Lord," and do not do what I say?' (Luke 6.46). James 1.25 warns us that the blessing does not come to us just from *knowing* God's will but from *doing* it. According to Ephesians 5.17 and 6.6, our Father wants us to understand his will and obey it from our hearts. Like Epaphras, we need to wrestle in prayer so that we might 'stand firm in all the will of God' (Col. 4.12).

Find what it is God wants you to do, that thing that he is waiting to bless in your life, the thing he has equipped you to do – and do it!

D. L. Moody lived for something essential – the will of God; and *he did something exceptional* – he obeyed the will of God. And because of this, *he received something eternal*. 'The man who does the will of God lives forever.'

We must not misunderstand the promise in this verse. John is not talking about immortality, because everybody will live forever either with God or apart from God. One day Jesus will welcome the sheep into the kingdom and send the goats away from his presence to the place prepared for the devil and his angels. No, the promise here is not that of immortality.

Nor is it a promise of perpetual reputation and honour. Many faithful servants of God have died and been forgotten, their names to be found only in footnotes in doctoral theses. Yet the names of many wicked sinners have been written indelibly on the pages of history and will never be forgotten. If you want to be entertained, find a copy of *Who Was Who* in the library and see how many of the names you recognize on its pages. During their lives, these people were famous and powerful, but today they are unknown.

When you read the context of Mr Moody's verse, you discover what the promise really involves.

Do not love the world or anything in the world. If anyone loves the world, the love of the Father is not in him. For everything in the world – the cravings of sinful man, the lust of his eyes and the boasting of what he has and does – comes not from the Father but from the world. The world and its desires pass away, but the man who does the will of God lives forever.

The contrast is between living for the shallow pleasures of a passing world and living for the lasting joys of an eternal God, between wasting your life on the temporary or investing your life in the eternal. Do Christians ever live for this passing world? Well, John wrote this letter to Christian people, so some of them must have been guilty. One of the saddest statements in Paul's last letter is, 'Demas, because he loved this world, has deserted me' (2 Tim. 4.10). If Demas wanted to enjoy the world today, he probably would not have to leave our churches. So much of the world has crept in, he might feel right at home! Yet everything Demas lived for has vanished and can never be recovered. How sad it is when we satisfy our desires and waste our lives on the temporary.

In the only recorded psalm we have from Moses, Psalm 90, he contrasted the fleeting world and the eternal God. Human life is like the grass that grows up in the morning and withers and dies at evening. We quickly return to the dust. Our days and nights come and go as swiftly as soldiers reporting for guard duty. But the last words of Moses in this doleful psalm are in the form of a prayer: 'Establish the work of our hands for us – yes, establish the work of our hands' (v. 17). That is an Old Testament version of 1 John 2.17.

Many years ago in our Youth for Christ rallies, we used to sing a little chorus that ought to be revived for today's young people:

> With eternity's values in view, Lord,
> With eternity's values in view,
> Let me do each day's work for Jesus,
> With eternity's values in view.

That's the meaning of 1 John 2.17.

When doing the will of God is the most important thing in our lives, then God will answer the prayer Moses wrote centuries ago, and he will fulfil the promise he gave to John. He did this for Mr Moody and he will do it for us. We will not waste our lives or merely spend our lives; we will invest our lives in that which is eternal. What we do will abide forever. It's what Jim Elliot wrote in his journal on 28 October 1949, 'He is no fool who gives what he cannot keep to gain what he cannot lose.'

During the 1875 campaign in Birmingham, England, D. L. Moody met R. W. Dale, at that time Great Britain's leading Congregational preacher and theologian. Commenting on the campaign, Dale said to Moody, 'This work is most plainly of God, for I can see no real relation between you and what you have done.' Moody laughed and replied that he should be very sorry if it were otherwise.

'The man who does the will of God lives forever.'

Will you be that man? Will you be that woman?

IO

ONE SERMON WAS ENOUGH: A FAMILY'S TESTIMONY

Richard Thomas Bewes

The preacher of the century, D. L. Moody, was at the height of his power, aged forty-five, when he arrived in England for a whirlwind campaign in the fall of 1882. One of his sermons, just one, was enough to tip several generations of the Bewes family in the direction of the Gospel and the Bible – beginning with my grandpa.

Thomas Bewes was fourteen, youngest of twelve in a solicitor's family in Plymouth, on England's south coast. How did Tommy get to the Drill Hall on that Tuesday night, 26 September? For none of the family went with him. Evy, his older believing sister, might have taken him, but she was away from home. It seems it was the household parlour-maid who accompanied the teenager to hear Moody and Sankey ... and we have never been able to trace her name.

'This way to Mr Moody's Mission', read the placards in Plymouth. Citadel Road was busy as people hurried to the Drill Hall for the seven o'clock start. 'Quite an hour earlier the place began to fill', reported the *Western Morning News*, 'so that by seven all the space in the building, with the exception of a few back seats in the gallery, was occupied.' An opening hymn was announced. 'I want the people to learn that chorus', declared Moody, 'it is very simple. I will ask the choir to sing the verses, and we will all sing the chorus.' Presently over three thousand people were singing:

> And take me as I am!
> And take me as I am!

> My only plea –
> Christ died for me,
> Oh, take me as I am!

The exercise was repeated. Moody raised a laugh by asking, 'All to sing – ministers and reporters too.'

Another hymn followed, and then prayer was led by the Vicar of St Jude's Church, Southsea, the Revd T. H. Howard. Two solos followed by Ira D. Sankey, which included his famous 'The Ninety and Nine'. He was accompanying himself on a sweet-tone American organ. He was, according to the reporter, 'in splendid voice, and sang this touching hymn with solemnising effect'. A further hymn, and it was time for the sermon.

Tommy was riveted throughout. At the end, as the crowd spilled out onto Cidadel Road, he had already made the decision that was to affect his future and that of us later generations in the Bewes family. We still possess the letter that he wrote to his sister Evy on the Friday of that week:

> Home Lodge, Mannamead, Plymouth
>
> My dear Evy,
>
>   Thank you very much for your letter. I am writing to tell you some good news which you will be glad to hear. I went to one of Moody's and Sankey's meetings on Tuesday, and there *I was saved*. He spoke from the 9th verse of the 3rd of Genesis. It is where art thou. He said that that was the first question that God ever asked man in the Bible, and that it was the first question that people ought to ask themselves and he said that there were two more that he was going to speak about and they were, Where are you going? and How are you going to spend eternity? I don't think he could have chosen better ones. Thank you very much for praying for me. . . . Please to excuse my writing very often as I can't find much time. I remain your loving brother,
>
> Tommy
> Friday 29

Perhaps it could be argued that D. L. Moody's words at the close of his address that Tuesday night had a prophetic tinge to them. The *Western Morning News* reported the next day:

> At the close of the sermon there was silent prayer, and as the hushed audience bowed their heads Mr Moody pleaded with those

among them who desired prayer to stand up for a moment and then resume their seats. Several persons, after a brief space, accepted the invitation. Now a young man would rise, and then a young woman, followed, perhaps, immediately afterward by her friend. As one man after another got up, Mr Moody said, 'I am glad to see so many young men getting up. God bless them.' Then, as there would be a pause in the risings, Mr Moody would urge his hearers to accept the opportunity of obtaining the benefit of the prayers of the Christians present. 'There must be hundreds,' he said; 'Why not rise at once?' Again, as one or two intelligent looking young men rose, Mr Moody said, 'I am so thankful to see these young men rise. They may have forty or fifty years of life before them, and what a great deal they can do for God in that time.'

And so it proved to be. Thomas Bewes went on to study at Corpus Christi College in Cambridge University, and from there to Ridley Hall Theological College, whose principal was then the famous Handley Moule, later to become Bishop of Durham. Tommy was to serve in the ordained ministry of the Anglican Church, and later helped to found the Rochester Diocesan Evangelical Union. In the event he was given over fifty years of active evangelical ministry.

His eldest son, Cecil, who was to be my father, also studied at Cambridge, and similarly at Ridley Hall, before ordination and subsequent service as a missionary in East Africa, together with responsibilities in the famed Keswick Convention. Numbers of Tommy's grandchildren were to enter upon full-time Christian service, and now I am a preaching grandfather myself, just one of a family of preachers.

Only one sermon among hundreds. Just one face among thousands. We, the descendants of Thomas Bewes, are happy to pay tribute to the effectiveness of God's Word preached, several generations down the line. To God be all the glory; the credit must be His. And I'm sure that's the way Moody would have had it too.

APPENDIX

D. L. MOODY:
A PERSONAL TRIBUTE

Henry Drummond

[Editor's Note: Henry Drummond, who was born in Stirling, Scotland, in 1851, became one of Moody's closest collaborators and dearest friends. His final year as a theological student at New College, Edinburgh, coincided with the first Moody–Sankey Evangelistic Campaign in Scotland (1873–4). Moody recruited Drummond to work in youth meetings and with follow-up activities and thus began a lifelong partnership between two unlikely allies: the plain-spoken, rough-hewn evangelist from Chicago, and the dapper, polished student of Edinburgh (and later professor at Glasgow). In the twilight of the late Victorian era, Drummond was a liminal figure who traversed the worlds of science and religion, reason and revelation, the academy and the church. He left an indelible impression on the latter half of the nineteenth century as an evangelist, scientist, teacher, writer, explorer and Christian apologist. He made three visits to America (1879, 1887, 1893), speaking to Ivy League students and faculties as well as to the large summer conferences sponsored by Moody at Northfield. What follows is a personal tribute to Moody written by Drummond in 1894 shortly after his last visit to America. Originally published under the title, 'Mr Moody: Some Impressions and Facts', it appeared in *McClure's Magazine* 4 (1894–95): 55–69, 188–92. Shortly after Moody's death in 1899, it was republished with an introduction by George Adam Smith as *Dwight L. Moody: Impressions and Facts* by Henry Drummond (New York: McClure, Phillips, 1900). Drummond's personal devotion to Moody and his defence of the ministry of the great evangelist was reciprocated by the older man. At Drummond's death, Moody wrote: 'No man has ever been with me for any length of time, but I could see some things in him that were unlike Christ, and I often see them in myself; but I never saw them in Henry Drummond. He is the most Christ-like man I ever knew.']

THE FIRST IMPRESSION

To gain just the right impression of Mr Moody you must make a pilgrimage to Northfield. Take the train to the wayside depot in Massachusetts which bears that name, or, better still, to South Vernon, where the fast trains stop. Northfield, his birthplace and his home, is distant about a couple of miles, but at certain seasons of the year you will find awaiting trains a two-horse buggy, not conspicuous for varnish, but famous for pace, driven by a stout, farmer-like person in a slouch hat. As he drives you to the spacious hotel – a creation of Mr Moody's – he will answer your questions about the place in a brusque, business-like way; indulge, probably, in a few laconic witticisms, or discuss the political situation or the last strike with a shrewdness which convinces you that, if the Northfield people are of this level-headed type, they are at least a worthy field for the great preacher's energies. Presently, on the other side of the river, on one of those luscious, grassy slopes, framed in with forest and bounded with the blue receding hills, which give the Connecticut Valley its dream-like beauty, the great halls and colleges of the new Northfield which Mr Moody has built begin to appear. Your astonishment is great, not so much to find a New England hamlet possessing a dozen of the finest educational buildings in America – for the neighbouring townships of Amherst and Northampton are already famous for their collegiate institutions – but to discover that these owe their existence to a man whose name is, perhaps, associated in the minds of three-fourths of his countrymen, not with education, but with the want of it. But presently, when you are deposited at the door of the hotel, a more astounding discovery greets you. For when you ask the clerk whether the great man himself is at home, and where you can see him, he will point to your coach-man, now disappearing like lightning down the drive, and – too much accustomed to Mr Moody's humour to smile at his latest jest – whisper, 'That's him.'

If this does not actually happen in your case it is certain it has happened;* and nothing could more fittingly introduce you to the man, or make you realize the naturalness, the simplicity, the genuine and unaffected humanity of this great unspoilt and unspoilable personality.

Simple as this man is, and homely as are his surroundings, probably America possesses at this moment no more extraordinary personage; nor even among the most brilliant of her sons has any rendered more stupendous or more enduring service to his country or his time. No public man is less understood, especially by the thinking world, than D. L. Moody. It is not that it is unaware of his existence, or even that it does not respect him. But his line is so special, his work has lain so apart from what it conceives to be the rational channels of progress, that it has never felt called upon to take him seriously. So little, indeed, is the true stature of this man known to the mass of his generation, that the preliminary estimate recorded here must seem both extravagant and ill-considered. To whole sections of the community the mere word evangelical is a synonym for whatever is narrow, strained, superficial and unreal. Assumed to be heir to all that is hectic in religion and sensational in the methods of propagating it, men who, like Mr Moody, earn this name are unconsciously credited with the worst traditions of their class. It will surprise many to know that Mr Moody is as different from the supposed type of his class as light is from dark; that while he would be the last to repudiate the name, indeed, while glorying more and more each day he lives in the

* At the beginning of each of the terms, hundreds of students, many of them strangers, arrive to attend those seminaries. At such times Mr Moody literally haunts the depots, to meet them the moment they most need a friend, and give them that personal welcome which is more to many of them than half their education. When casual visitors, mistaking perhaps the only vehicle in waiting for a public conveyance, have taken possession for themselves and their luggage, the driver, circumstances permitting, has duly risen to the occasion. The fact, by the way, that he so escapes recognition, illustrates a peculiarity – Mr Moody, owing to a life-long resistance to the self-advertisement of the camera, is probably less known by photographs than any other public man.

work of the evangelist, he sees the weaknesses, the narrownesses and the limitations of that order with as clear an eye as the most unsparing of its critics. But especially will it surprise many to know that while preaching to the masses has been the main outward work of Mr Moody's life, he has, perhaps, more, and more varied, irons in the fire – educational, philanthropic, religious – than almost any living man; and that vast as has been his public service as a preacher to the masses, it is probably true that his personal influence and private character have done as much as his preaching to affect his day and generation.

Discussion has abounded lately as to the standards by which a country shall judge its great men. And the verdict has been given unanimously on behalf of moral influence. Whether estimated by the moral qualities which go to the making up of his personal character, or the extent to which he has impressed these upon whole communities of men on both sides of the Atlantic, there is, perhaps, no more truly great man living than D. L. Moody. By moral influences in this connection I do not mean in any restricted sense religious influence. I mean the influence which, with whatever doctrinal accompaniments, or under whatever ecclesiastical flag, leads men to better lives and higher ideals; the influence which makes for noble character, personal enthusiasm, social well-being and national righteous-ness. I have never heard him quoted as a theologian. But I have met multitudes, and personally know, in large numbers, men and women of all churches and creeds, of many countries and ranks, from the poorest to the richest, and from the most ignorant to the most wise, upon whom he has placed an ineffaceable moral mark. There is no large town in Great Britain or Ireland, and I perceive there are few in America, where this man has not gone, where he has not lived for days, weeks or months, and where he has not left behind him personal inspirations which live to this day; inspirations which, from the moment of their birth, have not ceased to evidence themselves in practical ways – in furthering domestic happiness and peace; in charities and philanthropies; in social, religious and even municipal and national service.

It is no part of the present object to give a detailed account of Mr Moody's career, still less of his private life. The sacred character of much of his work also forbids allusion in this brief sketch to much that those more deeply interested in him, and in the message which he proclaims, would like to have expressed or analysed. All that is designed is to give the outside reader some few particulars to introduce him to, and interest him in, the man.

A New England boyhood

Fifty-seven years ago (5 February 1837) Dwight Lyman Moody was born in the same New England valley where, as already said, he lives today. Four years later his father died, leaving a widow, nine children – the eldest but thirteen years of age – a little home on the mountain side, and an acre or two of mortgaged land. How this widow shouldered her burden of poverty, debt and care; how she brought up her helpless flock, keeping all together in the old home, educating them and sending them out into life stamped with her own indomitable courage and lofty principle, is one of those unrecorded histories whose page, when time unfolds it, will be found to contain the secret of nearly all that is greatest in the world's past. It is delightful to think that this mother has survived to see her labours crowned, and still lives, a venerable and beautiful figure, near the scene of her early battles. There, in a sunny room of the little farm, she sits with faculties unimpaired, cherished by an entire community and surrounded with all the love and gratitude which her children and her children's children can heap upon her. One has only to look at the strong, wise face, or listen to the firm yet gentle tones, to behold the source of those qualities of sagacity, energy, self-unconsciousness and faith which have made the greatest of her sons what he is. Until his seventeenth year Mr Moody's boyhood was spent at home. What a merry, adventurous, rough-and-tumble boyhood it must have been, how much fuller of escapade than of education, those who know Mr Moody's irresistible temperament and buoyant humour will not require the traditions of his Northfield schoolmates to recall. The village school was the only seminary he ever attended, and his course was constantly interrupted by the duties of the home and of the farm. He learned little about books, but much about horses, crops and men; his mind ran wild, and his memory stored up nothing but the alphabet of knowledge. But in these early country days his bodily form strengthened to iron, and he built up that constitution which in after life enabled him not only to do the work of ten, but to sustain without break through four decades as arduous and exhausting work as was ever given to man to do. Innocent at this stage of 'religion', he was known in the neighbourhood simply as a raw lad, high-spirited, generous, daring, with a will of his own, and a certain audacious originality which, added to the fiery energy of his disposition, foreboded a probable future either in the ranks of the incorrigibles or, if fate were kind, perchance of the immortals.

Somewhere about his eighteenth year the turning-point came. Vast as were the issues, the circumstances were in no way eventful. Leaving school, the boy had set out for Boston, where he had an uncle, to push his fortune. His uncle, with some trepidation, offered him a place in his store; but, seeing the kind of nature he had to deal with, laid down certain conditions which the astute man thought might at least minimize explosions. One of these conditions was that the lad should attend church and Sunday school. These influences – and it is interesting to note that they are simply the normal influences of a Christian society – did their work. On the surface what appears is this: that he attended church – in order, and listened with more or less attention; that he went to Sunday school, and, when he recovered his breath, asked awkward questions of his teacher; that, by and by, when he applied for membership in the congregation, he was summarily rejected, and told to wait six months until he learned a little more about it; and, lastly, that said period of probation having expired, he was duly received into communion. The decisive instrument during this period seems to have been his Sunday-school teacher, Mr Edward Kimball, whose influence upon his charge was not merely professional, but personal and direct. In private friendship he urged young Moody to the supreme decision, and Mr Moody never ceased to express his gratitude to the layman who met him at the parting of the ways, and led his thoughts and energies in the direction in which they have done such service to the world.

The immediate fruit of this change was not specially apparent. The ambitions of the lad chiefly lay in the line of mercantile success; and his next move was to find a larger and freer field for the abilities for business which he began to discover in himself. This he found in the then new world of Chicago. Arriving there, with due introductions, he was soon engaged as salesman in a large and busy store, with possibilities of work and promotion which suited his taste. That he distinguished himself almost at once goes without saying. In a year or two he was earning a salary considerable for one of his years, and his business capacity became speedily so proved that his future prosperity was assured. 'He would never sit down in the store,' writes one of his fellows, 'to chat or read the paper, as the other clerks did when there were no customers; but as soon as he had served one buyer he was on the lookout for another. If none appeared he would start off to the hotels or depots, or walk the streets in search of one. He would sometimes stand on the sidewalk in front of his place of business, looking eagerly up and down for a man who had the appearance of a merchant from the country, and some of his fellow clerks were accustomed laughingly to say: "There is the spider again, watching for a fly."'

The taunt is sometimes levelled at religion that mainly those become religious teachers who are not fit for anything else. The charge is not worth answering; but it is worth recording that in the case of Mr Moody the very reverse is the case. If Mr Moody had remained in business, there is almost no question that he would have been today one of the wealthiest men in the United States. His enterprise, his organizing power, his knowledge and management of men are admitted by friend and foe to be of the highest order; while such is his generalship – as proved, for example, in the great religious campaign in Great Britain in 1873–5 – that, had he chosen a military career, he would have risen to the first rank among leaders. One of the merchant princes of Britain, the well-known director of one of the largest steamship companies in the world, assured the writer lately that in the course of a lifelong commercial experience he had never met a man with more business capacity and sheer executive ability than D. L. Moody. Let any one visit Northfield with its notable piles of institutions, or study the history of the work conceived, directed, financed and carried out on such a colossal scale by Mr Moody during the time of the World's Fair at Chicago, and he will discover for himself the size, the mere intellectual quality, creative power and organizing skill of the brain behind them.

Undiverted, however, from a deeper purpose even by the glamour of a successful business life, Mr Moody's moral and religious instincts led him almost from the day of his arrival in Chicago to devote what spare time he had to the work of the Church. He began by hiring four pews in the church to which he had attached himself, and these he attempted to fill every Sunday with young men like himself. This work for a temperament like his soon proved too slow, and he sought fuller outlets for his enthusiasm. Applying for the post of teacher in an obscure Sunday school, he was told by the superintendent that it was scholars he wanted, not teachers, but that he would let him try his hand if he could find the scholars. Next Sunday the new candidate appeared with a procession of eighteen urchins, ragged, rowdy and barefoot, on whom he straightway proceeded to operate. Hunting up children and general recruiting for mission halls remained favourite pursuits for years to come, and his success was signal. In all this class of work he was a natural adept, and his early experiences as a scout were full of adventure. This was probably the most picturesque period of Mr Moody's life, and not the least useful. Now we find him tract-distributing in the slums; again, visiting among the docks; and, finally, he started a mission of his own in one of the lowest haunts of the city. There he saw life in all its phases; he learned what practical religion was; he tried in succession every known method of Christian work; and when any of the conventional methods failed, invented new ones. Opposition, discouragement, failure he met at every turn and in every form; but one thing he never learned – how to give up man or scheme he had once set his heart on. For years this guerilla work, hand to hand, and heart to heart, went on. He ran through the whole gamut of mission experience, tackling the most difficulty districts and the most adverse circumstances, doing all the odd jobs and menial work himself, never attempting much in the way of public speaking, but employing others whom he thought more fit; making friends especially with children, and through them with their dissolute fathers and starving mothers.

Great as was his success, the main reward achieved was to the worker himself. Here he was broken in, moulded, toned down, disciplined, in a dozen needed directions, and in this long and severe apprenticeship he unconsciously qualified himself to become the teacher of the Church in all methods of reaching the masses and winning men. He found out where his strength lay, and where his weakness; he learned that saving men was no child's play, but meant practically giving a life for a life; that regeneration was no milk-and-water experience; that, as Mrs Browning says:

> It takes a high-soul'd man
> To move the masses – even to a cleaner sty.

But for this personal discipline it is doubtful if Mr Moody would ever have been heard of outside the purlieus of Chicago. The clergy, bewildered by his eccentric genius, and suspicious of his unconventional ways, looked askance at him; and it was only as time mellowed his headstrong youth into a soberer, yet not less zealous, manhood that the solitary worker found influential friends to countenance and guide him. He became at last a recognized factor in the religious life of Chicago. The mission which he had slowly built up was elevated to the rank of a church, with Mr Moody, who had long since given up business in order to devote his entire time to what lay nearer his heart, as its pastor.

HIS EARLY CHURCH WORK

As a public speaker up to this time Mr Moody was the reverse of celebrated. When he first attempted speaking, in Boston, he was promptly told to hold his tongue, and further efforts in Chicago were not less discouraging. 'He had never heard,' writes Mr Daniels, in his well-known biography, 'of Talley-rand's famous doctrine, that speech is useful for concealing one's thoughts. Like Antony, he only spoke "right on". There was frequently a pungency in his exhortation which his brethren did not altogether relish. Sometimes in his prayers he would express opinions to the Lord concerning them which were by no means flattering; and it was not long before he received the same fatherly advice which had been given him at Boston – to the effect that he should keep his four pews full of young men, and leave the speaking and praying to those who could do it better.' Undaunted by such pleasantries, Mr Moody did, on occasion, continue to use his tongue – no doubt much ashamed of himself. He spoke not because he thought he could speak, but because he could not be silent. The ragged children whom he gathered round him in the empty saloon near the North Side Market, had to be talked to somehow, and among such audiences, with neither premeditation nor preparation, he laid the foundations of that amazingly direct anecdotal style and explosive delivery which became such a splendid instrument of his future service. Training for the public platform this man who has done more platform work than any man of his generation had none. He knew only two books, the Bible and Human Nature. Out of these he spoke; and because both are books of life, his words were afire with life; and the people to whom he spoke, being real people, listened and understood. When Mr Moody first began to be in demand on public platforms, it was not because he could speak. It was his experience that was wanted, not his eloquence. As a practical man in work among the masses, his advice and enthusiasm were called for at Sunday school and other conventions, and he soon became known in this connection throughout the surrounding States. It was at one of these conventions that he had the good fortune to meet Mr Ira D. Sankey, whose name must ever be associated with his, and who henceforth shared his labours at home and abroad, and contributed, in ways the value of which it is impossible to exaggerate, to the success of his after work.

Were one asked what, on the human side, were the effective ingredients in Mr Moody's sermons, one would find the answer difficult. Probably the foremost is the tremendous conviction with which they are uttered. Next to that is their point and direction. Every blow is straight from the shoulder, and every stroke tells. Whatever canon they violate, whatever fault the critics may find with their art, their rhetoric, or even with their theology, as appeals to the people they do their work, and with extraordinary power. If eloquence is measured by its effects upon an audience, and cumulative periods, then here is eloquence of the highest order. In sheer persuasiveness Mr Moody has few equals, and rugged as his preaching may seem to some, there is in it a pathos of a quality which few orators have ever reached, an appealing tenderness which not only wholly redeems it, but raises it, not unseldom almost to sublimity. No report can do the faintest justice to this or to the other most characteristic qualities of his public speech, but here is a specimen taken almost at random: 'I can imagine when Christ said to the little band around Him, "Go ye into all the world and preach the gospel," Peter said, "Lord, do you really mean that we are to go back to Jerusalem and preach the gospel to those men that murdered you?" "Yes," said Christ, "go, hunt up that man that spat in my face, tell him he may have a seat in my kingdom yet. Yes, Peter, go find that man that made that cruel crown of thorns and placed it on my brow, and tell him I will have a crown ready for him when he comes into my kingdom, and there will be no thorns in it. Hunt up that man that took a reed and brought it down over the cruel thorns, driving them into my brow, and tell him I will put a sceptre in his hand, and he shall rule over the nations of the earth, if he will accept salvation as a gift." ' *Tell him there is a nearer way to my heart than that* – prepared or impromptu, what dramatist could surpass the touch?

His method of sermon-making is original. In reality his sermons are never made, they are always still in the making. Suppose the subject is Paul: he takes a monstrous envelope capable of holding some hundreds of slips of paper, labels it 'Paul', and slowly stocks it with original notes, cuttings from papers, extracts from books, illustrations, scraps of all kinds, nearly or remotely referring to the subject. After accumulating these, it may be for years, he wades through the mass, selects a number of the most striking points, arranges them, and, finally, makes a few jottings in a large hand, and these he carries with him to the platform. The process of looking through the whole envelope is repeated each time the sermon is preached. Partly on this account, and partly because in delivery he forgets some points, or disproportionately amplifies others, no two sermons are ever exactly the same. By this method also – a matter of much more importance – the delivery is always fresh to himself. Thus, to make this clearer, suppose that after a thorough sifting, one hundred eligible points remain in the envelope. Every time the sermon is preached, these hundred are overhauled. But no single sermon, by a mere limitation of time, can contain, say, more than seventy. Hence, though the general scheme is the same, there is always novelty both in the subject matter and in the arrangement, for the particular seventy varies with each time of delivery. No greater mistake could be made than to imagine that Mr Moody does not study for his sermons. On the contrary, he is always studying. When in the evangelistic field, the batch of envelopes, bursting with fatness, appears the moment breakfast is over; and the stranger who enters at almost any time of day, except at the hours of platform work, will find him with his litter of notes, either stuffing himself or his port-folios with the new 'points' he has picked up through the day. His search for these 'points', and especially for light upon texts, Bible ideas, or characters, is ceaseless, and he has an eye like an eagle for anything really good. Possessing a considerable library, he browses over it when at home; but his books are chiefly men, and no student ever read the ever-open page more diligently, more intelligently, or to more immediate practical purpose.

To Mr Moody himself it has always been a standing marvel that people should come to hear him. He honestly believes that ten thousand sermons are made every week, in obscure towns, and by unknown men, vastly better than anything he can do. All he knows about his own productions is that somehow they achieve the result intended. No man is more willing to stand aside and let others speak. His search for men to whom the people will listen, for men who, whatever the meagreness of their message, can yet hold an audience, has been lifelong, and whenever and wherever he finds such men he instantly seeks to employ them. The word jealousy he has never heard. At one of his own conventions at Northfield he has been known to keep silent – but for the exercise of the duties of chairman – during almost the whole ten days' sederunt, while mediocre men – I speak comparatively, not disrespectfully – were pushed to the front.

It is at such conferences, by the way, no matter in what part of the world they are held, that one discovers Mr Moody's size. He gathers round him the best men he can find, and very good men most of them are; but when one comes away, it is always

Mr Moody that one remembers. It is he who leaves the impress upon us; his word and spirit live; the rest of us are forgotten and forget one another. It is the same story when on the evangelistic round. In every city the prominent workers in that field for leagues around are all in evidence. They crowd round the central figure like bees; you can review the whole army at once. And it is no disparagement to the others to say – what each probably feels for himself – that so high is the stature and commanding personality of Mr Moody that there seems to be but one real man among them, one character untarnished by intolerance or pettiness, pretentiousness or self-seeking. He makes mistakes like others; but in largeness of heart, in breadth of view, in single-eyedness and humility, in teachableness and self-obliteration, in sheer goodness and love, none can stand beside him.

HIS WORLD MINISTRY

After the early Chicago days, the most remarkable episode in Mr Moody's career was his preaching tour in Great Britain. The burning down of his church in Chicago severed the tie which bound him to the city, and though he still retained a connection with it, his ministry henceforth belonged to the world. Leaving his mark on Chicago, in many directions – on missions, churches, and, not least, on the Young Men's Christian Association – and already famous in the West for his success in evangelical work, he arrived in England, with his colleague Mr Sankey, in June 1873. The opening of their work there was not auspicious. Two of the friends who had invited them had died, and the strangers had an uphill fight. No one had heard of them; the organ and the solos of Mr Sankey were an innovation sufficient to ruin almost any cause. For some time the prospect was bleak enough. In the town of Newcastle finally some faint show of public interest was awakened. One or two earnest ministers in Edinburgh went to see for themselves. On returning they reported cautiously, but on the whole favourably, to their brethren. The immediate result was an invitation to visit the capital of Scotland; and the final result was the starting of a religious movement, quiet, deep and lasting, which moved the country from shore to shore, spread to England, Wales and Ireland, and reached a climax two years later in London itself.

This is not the place, as already said, to enter either into criticism or into details of such a work. Like all popular movements it had its mistakes, its exaggerations, even its great dangers; but these were probably never less in any equally widespread movement of history, nor was the balance of good upon the whole ever greater, more solid or more enduring. People who understand by a religious movement only a promiscuous carnival of hysterical natures, beginning in excitement and ending in moral exhaustion and fanaticism, will probably be assured in vain that whatever were the lasting characteristics of this movement, these were not. That such elements were wholly absent may not be asserted; human nature is human nature; but always the first to fight them, on the rare occasions when they appeared, was Mr Moody himself. He, above all popular preachers, worked for solid results. Even the mere harvesting – his own special department – was a secondary thing to him compared with the garnering of the fruits by the Church and their subsequent growth and further fruitfulness. It was the writer's privilege as a humble camp-follower to follow the fortunes of this campaign personally from town to town, and from city to city, throughout the three kingdoms, for over a year. And time has only deepened the impression not only of the magnitude of the results immediately secured, but equally of the permanence of the after-effects upon every field of social, philanthropic and religious activity. It is not too much to say that Scotland – one can speak with less knowledge of England and Ireland – would not have been the same today but for the visit of Mr Moody and Mr Sankey; and that so far-reaching was, and is, the influence of their work, that any one who knows the inner religious history of the country must regard this time as nothing short of a national epoch. If this is a specimen of what has been effected even in less degree elsewhere, it represents a fact of commanding importance. Those who can speak with authority of the long series of campaigns which succeeded this in America, testify in many cases with almost equal assurance of the results achieved both throughout the United States and Canada.

After his return from Great Britain, in 1875, Mr Moody made his home at Northfield, his house in Chicago having been swept away by the fire. And from this point onward his activity assumed a new and extraordinary development. Continuing his evangelistic work in America, and even on one occasion revisiting England, he spent his intervals of repose in planning and founding the great educational institutions of which Northfield is now the centre.

There is no stronger proof of Mr Moody's breadth of mind than that he should have inaugurated this work. For an evangelist seriously to concern himself with such matters is unusual; but that the greatest evangelist of his day, not when his powers were failing, but in the prime of life and in the zenith of his success, should divert so great a measure of his strength into educational channels, is a phenomenal circumstance. The explanation is manifold. No man sees so much slip-shod, unsatisfactory and half-done work as the evangelist; no man so learns the worth of solidity, the necessity for a firm basis for religion to work upon, the importance to the Kingdom of God of men who 'weigh'. The value, above all things, of character, of the sound mind and disciplined judgement, are borne in upon him every day he lives. Converts without these are weak-kneed and useless; Christian workers inefficient, if not dangerous. Mr Moody saw that the object of Christianity was to make good men and good women – good men and good women who would serve their God and their country not only with all their heart, but with all their mind and all their strength. Hence he would found institutions for turning out such characters. His pupils should be committed to nothing as regards a future profession. They might become ministers or missionaries, evangelists or teachers, farmers or politicians, businessmen or lawyers. All that he would secure would be that they should have a chance – a chance of becoming useful, educated, God-fearing men. A favourite aphorism with him is, that 'it is better to set ten men to work than to do the work of ten men'. His institutions were founded to equip other men to work, not in the precise line, but in the same broad interest as himself. He himself had had the scantiest equipment for his life-work, and he daily lamented – though perhaps no one else ever did – the deficiency. In his journeys he constantly met young men and young women of earnest spirit, with circumstances against them, who were in danger of being lost to themselves and to the community. These especially it was his desire to help, and afford a chance in life. 'The motive,' says the *Official Handbook*, 'presented for the pursuit of an education is the power it confers for Christian life and usefulness, not the means it affords to social distinction, or the gratification of selfish ambition. It is designed to combine, with other instruction, an unusual amount of instruction in the Bible, and it is intended that all the training shall exhibit a thoroughly Christian spirit. . . . No constraint is placed on the religious view of any one. . . . The chief emphasis of the instruction given is placed upon the life.'

The plan, of course, developed by degrees, but once resolved upon, the beginning was made with characteristic decision; for the years other men spend in criticizing a project, Mr Moody spends in executing it. One day in his own house, talking with Mr H. N. F. Marshall about the advisability of immediately securing a piece of property – some sixteen acres close to his door – his friend expressed his assent. The words were scarcely uttered when the owner of the land was seen walking along the road. He was invited in, the price fixed, and, to the astonishment of the owner, the papers made out on the spot. Next winter a second lot was bought, the building of a seminary for female students commenced, and at the present moment the land in connection with this one institution amounts to over two hundred and seventy acres. The current expense of this one school per annum is over fifty-one thousand dollars, thirty thousand dollars of which comes from the students themselves; and the existing endowment, the most of which, however, is not yet available, reaches one hundred and four thousand dollars. Dotted over the noble campus thus secured, and clustered especially near Mr Moody's home, stand ten spacious buildings and a number of smaller size, all connected with the Ladies' Seminary. The education, up to the standard aimed at, is of first-rate quality, and prepares students for entrance into Wellesley and other institutions of similar high rank.

Four miles distant from the Ladies' Seminary, on the rising ground on the opposite side of the river, are the no less imposing buildings of the Mount Hermon School for Young Men.

Conceived earlier than the former, but carried out later, this institution is similar in character, though many of the details are different. Its three or four hundred students are housed in ten fine buildings, with a score of smaller ones. Surrounding the whole is a great farm of two hundred and seventy acres, farmed by the pupils themselves. This economic addition to the educational training of the students is an inspiration of Mr Moody's. Nearly every pupil is required to do from an hour and a half to two hours and a half of farm or industrial work each day, and much of the domestic work is similarly distributed. The lads work on the roads, in the fields, in the woods; in the refectory, laundry and kitchen; they take charge of the horses, the cattle, the hogs and the hens – for the advantage of all which the sceptical may be referred to Mr Ruskin. Once or twice a year nearly everyone's work is changed; the indoor lads go out, the farm lads come in. Those who before entering the school had already learned trades, have the opportunity of pursuing them in leisure hours and, though the industrial department is strongly subordinated to the educational, many in this way help to pay the fee of one hundred dollars exacted annually from each pupil which pays for tuition, board, rooms, etc.

The mention of this fee – which, it may be said in passing, only covers half the cost – suggests the question as to how the vast expenses of these and other institutions, such as the new Bible Institute in Chicago, and the Bible, sewing and cooking school into which the Northfield Hotel is converted in winter, are defrayed. The buildings themselves and the land have been largely the gift of friends, but much of the cost of maintenance is paid out of Mr Moody's own pocket. The fact that Mr Moody has a pocket has been largely dwelt upon by his enemies, and the amount and source of its contents are subjects of curious speculation. I shall suppose the critic to be honest, and divulge to him a fact which the world has been slow to learn – the secret of Mr Moody's pocket. It is briefly, that Mr Moody is the owner of one of the most paying literary properties in existence. It is the hymnbook which, first used at his meetings in conjunction with Mr Sankey, whose genius created it, is now in universal use throughout the civilized world. Twenty years ago, he offered it for nothing to a dozen different publishers, but none of them would look at it. Failing to find a publisher, Mr Moody, with almost the last few dollars he possessed, had it printed in London in 1873. The copyright stood in his name; any loss that might have been suffered was his; and to any gain, by all the laws of business, he was justly entitled. The success, slow at first, presently became gigantic. The two evangelists saw a fortune in their hymnbook. But they saw something which was more vital to them than a fortune – that the busybody and the evil tongue would accuse them, if they but touched one cent of it, of preaching the gospel for gain. What did they do? They refused to touch it – literally even to touch it. The royalty was handed direct from the publishers to a committee of well-known businessmen in London, who distributed it to various charities. When the evangelists left London, a similar committee, with Mr W. E. Dodge at its head, was formed in New York. For many years this committee faithfully disbursed the trust, and finally handed over its responsibility to a committee of no less weight and honour – the trustees of the Northfield seminaries, to be used henceforth in their behalf. Such is the history of Mr Moody's pocket. It is pitiful to think that there are men and journals, both at home and abroad, who continue to accuse of self-seeking a man who had given up a princely fortune in noble – the man of the world would say superfluous – jealousy for the mission of his life. Once we heard far more of this. That Mr Moody has lived it down is not the least of his triumphs.

His training school

In the year 1889 Mr Moody broke out in a new place. Not content with having founded two great schools at Northfield, he turned his attention to Chicago, and inaugurated there one of his most successful enterprises – the Bible Institute. This scheme grew out of many years' thought. The general idea was to equip lay workers – men and women – for work among the poor, the outcast, the churchless and the illiterate. In every centre of population there is a call for such help. The demand for city missionaries, Bible readers, evangelists, superintendents of Christian and philanthropic institutions, is unlimited. In the foreign field it is equally clamant. Mr Moody saw that all over the country were those who, with a little special training, might become effective workers in these various spheres – some whose early opportunities had been neglected; some who were too old or too poor to go to college; and others who, half their time, had to earn their living. To meet such workers and such work the Institute was conceived.

The heart of Chicago, both morally and physically, offered a suitable site, and here, adjoining the Chicago Avenue Church, a preliminary purchase of land was made at a cost of fifty-five thousand dollars. On part of this land, for a similar sum, a three-storeyed building was put up to accommodate male students, while three houses, already standing on the property, were transformed into a ladies' department. No sooner were the doors opened than some ninety men and fifty women began to work. So immediate was the response that all the available accommodation was used up, and important enlargements have had to be made since. The mornings at the Institute are largely given up to Bible study and music, the afternoons to private study and visitation, and the evenings to evangelistic work. In the second year of its existence no fewer than two hundred and forty-eight students were on the roll-book. In addition to private study, these conducted over three thousand meetings, large and small, in the city and neighbourhood, paid ten thousand visits to the homes of the poor, and 'called in' at more than a thousand saloons.

As to the ultimate destination of the workers, the statistics for this same year record the following:

At work in India are three, one man and two women; in China, three men and one woman, with four more (sexes equally divided) waiting appointment there; in Africa two men and two women, with two men and one woman waiting appointment; in Turkey, one man and five women; in South America, one man and one woman; in Bulgaria, Persia, Burma and Japan, one woman to each. Among the North American Indians, three women and one man. In the home field, in America, are thirty-seven men and nine women employed in evangelistic work, thirty-one in pastoral work (including many ministers who had come for further study), and twenty-nine in other schools and colleges. Sunday-school missions employ five men; home missions, two; the Young Men's Christian Association, seven; the Young Women's Christian Association, two. Five men and one woman are 'singing evangelists'. Several have positions in charitable institutions, others are evangelists and twenty are teachers. It will be allowed that this is a pretty fair record for a two-years' old institute. As Mr Moody gives it much of his time, spending many months there annually in personal superintendence, there can be little doubt as to its future.

Not quite on the same lines, but with certain features in common, is still a fourth institution founded by the evangelist at Northfield about the same time. This is, perhaps, one of his most original developments – the Northfield Training School for Women. In his own work at Chicago, and in his evangelistic rounds among the churches, he had learned to appreciate the exceptional value of women in ministering to the poor. He saw, however, that women of the right stamp were not always to be found where they were needed most, and in many cases where they were to be found, their work was marred by inexperience and lack of training. He determined, therefore, to start a novel species of training school, which city churches and mission fields could draw upon, not for highly educated missionaries, but for Christian women who had undergone a measure of special instruction, especially in Bible knowledge and *domestic economy* – the latter being the special feature. The initial obstacle of a building in which to start his institute was no difficulty to Mr Moody. Among the many great buildings of Northfield there was one which, every winter, was an eyesore to him. It was the Northfield Hotel, and it was an eyesore because it was empty. After the busy season in summer, it was shut up from October till the end of March, and Mr Moody resolved that he would turn its halls into lecture rooms, its bedrooms into dormitories, stock the first with teachers, and the second with scholars, and start the work of the Training School as soon as the last guest was off the premises.

In October 1890, the first term opened. Six instructors were provided, and fifty-six students took up residence at once. Next year the numbers were almost doubled, and the hotel college today is in a fair way to become a large and important institution. In addition to systematic Bible study, which forms the backbone of the curriculum, the pupils are taught those branches of domestic economy which are most likely to be useful in their work among the homes of the poor. Much stress is laid upon cooking, especially the preparation of foods for the sick, and a distinct department is also devoted to dressmaking. An objection was raised at the outset that the students, during their term of residence, were isolated from the active Christian work in which their lives were to be spent, and that hence the most important part of their training must be merely theoretical. But this difficulty has solved itself. Though not contemplated at the founding of the school, the living energy and enthusiasm of the students have sought their own outlets; and now, all through the winter, flying columns may be found scouring the countryside in all directions, visiting the homesteads and holding services in hamlets, cottages and school houses.

Like all Mr Moody's institutions, the winter Training Home is undenominational and unsectarian. It is a peculiarity of Northfield that every door is open not only to the Church Universal, but to the world. Every State in the Union is represented among the students of his two great colleges, and almost every nation and race. On the college books are, or have been, Africans, Armenians, Turks, Syrians, Austrians, Hungarians, Canadians, Danes, Dutch, English, French, German, Indian, Irish, Japanese, Chinese, Norwegians, Russians, Scotch, Swedish, Alaskans and Bulgarians. These include every type of Christianity, members of every Christian denomination and disciples of every Christian creed. Twenty-two denominations, at least, have shared the hospitality of the schools. This, for a religious educational institution, is itself a liberal education; and that Mr Moody should not only have permitted, but encouraged, this cosmopolitan and unsectarian character, is a witness at once to his sagacity and to his breadth.

With everything in his special career, in his habitual environment, and in the traditions of his special work, to make him intolerant, Mr Moody's sympathies have only broadened with time. Some years ago the Roman Catholics in Northfield determined to build a church. They went round the township collecting subscriptions, and by and by approached Mr Moody's door. How did he receive them? The narrower evangelical would have shut the door in their faces, or opened it only to give them a lecture on the blasphemies of the Pope or the iniquities of the Scarlet Woman. Mr Moody gave them one of the handsomest subscriptions on their list. Not content with that, when their little chapel was finished, he presented them with an organ. 'Why,' he exclaimed, when some one challenged the action, 'if they are Roman Catholics, it is better they should be good Roman Catholics than bad. It is surely better to have a Catholic church than none; and as for the organ, if they are to have music in their church, it is better to have good music. Besides,' he added, 'these are my own townspeople. If ever I am to be of the least use to them, surely I must help them.' What the kindly feeling did for them it is difficult to say; but what it did for Mr Moody is matter of local history. For, a short time after, it was rumoured that he was going to build a church, and the site was pointed out by the villagers – a rocky knoll close by the present hotel. One day Mr Moody found the summit of this knoll covered with great piles of stones. The Roman Catholics had taken their teams up the mountain and brought down, as a return present, enough building-stone to form the foundations of his church.

Mr Moody's relations with the Northfield people and with all the people for miles and miles around are of the same type. So far from being without honour in his own country, it is there he is honoured most. This fact – and nothing more truly decisive of character can be said – may be verified even by the stranger on the [railroad] cars. The nearer he approaches Northfield, the more thorough and genuine will he find the appreciation of Mr Moody; and when he passes under Mr Moody's own roof, he will find it truest, surest and most affectionate of all. It is forbidden here to invade the privacy of Mr Moody's home. Suffice it to say that no more perfect homelife exists in the world, and that one only begins to know the greatness, the tenderness and the simple beauty of this man's character when one sees him at his own fireside. One evidence of this greatness it is difficult to omit recording. If you were to ask Mr Moody – which it would never occur to you to do – what, apart from the inspirations of his personal faith, was the secret of his success, of his happiness and usefulness in life, he would assuredly answer, 'Mrs Moody'.

Results of his work

When one has recorded the rise and progress of the four institutions which have been named, one but stands on the threshold of the history of the tangible memorials of Mr Moody's career. To realize even partially the intangible results of his life is not within the compass of man's power; but even the tangible results – the results which have definite visible outcome, which are capable of statistical expression, which can be seen in action in different parts of the world today – it would tax a diligent historian to tabulate. The sympathies and activities of men like D. L. Moody are supposed by many to be wasted on the empty air. It will surprise them to be told that he is probably responsible for more actual stone and lime than almost any man in the world. There is scarcely a great city in England where he has not left behind him some visible memorial. His progress through Great Britain and Ireland, now nearly twenty years ago, is marked today by halls, churches, institutes and other buildings which owe their existence directly to his influence. In the capital of each of these countries – in London, Edinburgh and Dublin – great buildings stand today which, but for him, had had no existence. In the city where these words are written, at least three important institutions, each the centre of much work and a multitude of workers, Christian philanthropy owes to him. Young Men's Christian Associations all over the land have been housed, and in many cases sumptuously housed, not only largely by his initiative, but by his personal actions in raising funds. Mr Moody is the most magnificent beggar Great Britain has ever known. He will talk over a millionaire in less time than it takes other men to apologize for intruding upon his time. His gift for extracting money amounts to genius. The hard, the sordid, the miserly, positively melt before him. But his power to deal with refractory ones is not the best of it. His supreme success is with the already liberal, with those who give, or think they give, handsomely already. These he somehow convinces that their givings are nothing at all; and there are multitudes of rich men in the world who would confess that Mr Moody inaugurated for them, and for their churches and cities, the day of large subscriptions. The process by which he works is, of course, a secret, but one-half of it probably depends upon two things. In the first place, his appeals are wholly for others; for places – I am speaking of England – in which he would never set foot again; for causes in which he had no personal stake. In the second place, he always knew the right moment to strike.

On one occasion, to recall an illustration of the last, he had convened a great conference in Liverpool. The theme for discussion was a favourite one – 'How to reach the masses.' One of the speakers, the Rev. Charles Garrett, in a powerful speech, expressed his conviction that the chief want of the masses in Liverpool was the institution of cheap houses of refreshment to counteract the saloons. When he had finished, Mr Moody called upon him to speak for ten minutes more. That ten minutes might almost be said to have been a crisis in the social history of Liverpool. Mr Moody spent it in whispered conversation with gentlemen on the platform. No sooner was the speaker done than Mr Moody sprang to his feet and announced that a company had been formed to carry out the objects Mr Garrett had advocated; that various gentlemen, whom he named (Mr Alexander Balfour, Mr Samuel Smith MP, Mr Lockhart and others), had each taken one thousand shares of five dollars each, and that the subscription list would be open till the end of the meeting. The capital was gathered almost before the adjournment, and a company floated under the name of the 'British Workman Company Limited', which has not only worked a small revolution in Liverpool, but – what was not contemplated or wished for, except as an index of healthy business – paid a handsome dividend to the shareholders. For twenty years this company has gone on increasing; its ramifications are in every quarter of the city; it has returned ten per cent throughout the whole period, except for one (strike) year, when it returned seven; and, above all, it has been copied by cities and towns innumerable all over Great Britain. To Mr Garrett, who unconsciously set the ball a-rolling, the personal consequences were as curious as they were unexpected. 'You must take charge of this thing,' said Mr Moody to him, 'or at least you must keep your eye on it.' 'That cannot be,' was the reply. 'I am a Wesleyan; my three years in Liverpool have expired; I must pass to another circuit.' 'No,' said Mr Moody, 'you must stay here.' Mr Garrett assured him it was quite impossible, the

Methodist Conference made no exceptions. But Mr Moody would not be beaten. He got up a petition to the Conference. It was granted – an almost unheard-of thing – and Mr Garrett remains in his Liverpool church to this day. This last incident proves at least one thing – that Mr Moody's audacity is at least equalled by his influence.

That I have not told one tithe that is due to the subject of this sketch, I painfully realize now that my space has narrowed to its close. It is of small significance that one should make out this or the other man to be numbered among the world's great. But it is of importance to national ideals that standards of worthiness should be truly drawn, and, when those who answer to them in real life appear, that they should be held up for the world's instruction. Mr Moody himself has never asked for justice, and never for homage. The criticism which sours, and the adulation – an adulation at epochs in his life amounting to worship – which spoils, have left him alike untouched. The way he turned aside from applause in England struck multitudes with wonder. To be courted was to him not merely a thing to be discouraged on general principles; it simply made him miserable. At the close of a great meeting, when crowds, not of the base, but of the worthy, thronged the platform to press his hand, somehow he had always disappeared. When they followed him to his hotel, its doors were barred. When they wrote him, as they did in thousands, they got no response. This man would not be praised. Yet, partly for this very reason, those who love him love to praise him. And I may as well confess what has induced me, against keen personal dislike to all that is personal, to write these reminiscences. One day, travelling in America last summer, a high dignitary of the Church in my presence made a contemptuous reference to Mr Moody. A score of times in my life I have sailed in on such occasions, and at least taught the detractor some facts. On this occasion, with due humility, I asked the speaker if he had ever met him. He had not; and the reply elicited that the name which he had used so lightly was to him no more than an echo. I determined that, time being then denied, I would take the first opportunity of bringing that echo nearer him. It is for him these words were written. In the *Life of Whittier*, just published, the patronizing reference to Mr Moody but too plainly confirms the statement with which I opened –

that few men were less known to their contemporaries. 'Moody and Sankey,' writes the poet, 'are busy in Boston. The papers give the discourses of Mr Moody, which seem rather commonplace and poor, but the man is in earnest. . . . I hope he will do good, and believe that he will reach and move some who could not be touched by James Freeman Clark or Phillips Brooks. I cannot accept his theology, or part of it at least, and his methods are not to my taste. But if he can make the drunkard, the gambler and the debauchee into decent men, and make the lot of their weariful wives and children less bitter, I bid him Godspeed.'

I have called these words patronizing, but the expression should be withdrawn. Whittier was incapable of that. They are broad, large-hearted, even kind. But they are not the right words. They are the stereotyped charities which sweet natures apply to anything not absolutely harmful, and contain no more impression of the tremendous intellectual and moral force of *the man behind* than if the reference were to the obscurest Salvation Army zealot. I shall not endorse, for it could only give offence, the remark of a certain author of worldwide repute when he read the words: 'Moody! Why, he could have put half a dozen Whittiers in his pocket, and they would never have been noticed'; but I shall endorse, and with hearty good will, a judgement which he further added. 'I have always held,' he said – and he is a man who has met every great contemporary thinker from Carlyle downward – 'that in sheer brainsize, in the mere raw material of intellect, Moody stands among the first three or four great men I have ever known.' I believe Great Britain is credited with having 'discovered' Mr Moody. It may or may not be; but if it be, it was men of the quality and the experience of my friend who made the discovery; and that so many distinguished men in America have failed to appreciate him is a circumstance which has only one explanation – that they have never had the opportunity.

An American estimate, nevertheless, meets my eye as I lay down the pen, which I gladly plead space for, as it proves that in Mr Moody's own country there are not wanting those who discern how much he stands for. They are the notes, slightly condensed, of one whose opportunities for judging of his life and work have been exceptionally wide. In his opinion:

1. No other living man has done so much directly in the way of uniting man to God, and in restoring men to their true centre.
2. No other living man has done so much to unite man with man, to break down personal grudges and ecclesiastical barriers, bringing into united worship and harmonious cooperation men of diverse views and dispositions.
3. No other living man has set so many other people to work, and developed, by awakening the sense of responsibility, latent talents and powers which would otherwise have lain dormant.
4. No other living man, by precept and example, has so vindicated the right, privileges and duties of laymen.
5. No other living man has raised more money for other people's enterprises.
6. No other evangelist has kept himself so aloof from fads, religious or otherwise; from isms, from special reforms, from running specific doctrines, or attacking specific sins; has so concentrated his life upon the one supreme endeavour.

If a quarter of this be true, it is a unique and noble record; if all be true, which of us is worthy even to characterize it?

SUGGESTED READING

Abbott, Lyman (1921) 'Snapshots of My Contemporaries: Dwight Lyman Moody – Evangelist', *The Outlook* 64 (22 June): 324–7.

Corts, Thomas E. (ed.) (1999) *Henry Drummond: A Perpetual Benediction*. Edinburgh: T & T Clark.

Curtis, Richard K. (1962) *They Called Him Mister Moody*. Grand Rapids, MI: Eerdmans.

Day, Richard Ellsworth (1936) *Bush Aglow: The Life Story of Dwight Lyman Moody, Commoner of Northfield*. Philadelphia: Judson.

Dorsett, Lyle W. (1997) *A Passion for Souls: The Life of D. L. Moody*. Chicago: Moody Press.

Evensen, Bruce, J. (2003) *God's Man for the Gilded Age: D. L. Moody and the Rise of Modern Mass Evangelism*. Oxford: Oxford University Press.

Farwell, John V. (1907) *Early Recollections of D. L. Moody*. Chicago: Winona Publishing.

Findlay, James F., Jr (1969) *Dwight L. Moody: American Evangelist, 1837–1899*. Chicago: University of Chicago Press.

George, Timothy (2003) 'Henry Drummond', *Biographical Dictionary of Evangelicals*, ed. Timothy Larsen. Leicester, England: InterVarsity Press.

—— (1999) 'Why We Still Need Moody', *Christianity Today* 43 (14) (6 December): 66.

Gordon, James M. (1991) 'Dwight L. Moody and Frances R. Havergal', *Evangelical Spirituality: From the Wesleys to John Stott*. London: SPCK.

Gundry, Stanley N. (1976) *Love Them In: The Proclamation Theology of D. L. Moody*. Chicago: Moody Press.

Kent, John (1978) *Holding the Fort: Studies in Victorian Revivalism*. London: Epworth Press.

McDowell, John *et al.* (1937) *What D. L. Moody Means to Me: An Anthology of Appreciations and Appraisals of the Beloved Founder of the Northfield Schools*. E. Northfield, MA: The Northfield Schools.

Miller, Donald, L. (1996) *City of the Century: The Epic of Chicago and the Making of America*. New York: Simon & Schuster.

Moody, Paul Dwight (1963) *My Father: A Biographical Portrait of the Pacesetter in Modern Mass Evangelism*. New York: Macmillan.

Moody, William R. (1930) *The Life of D. L. Moody*. New York: Macmillan.

Pollock, John C. (1962) 'Dwight L. Moody – Grandfather of Ecumenism?' *Christianity Today* 7 (23 November): 29–30 [189–90].

—— (1963) *Moody: A Biographical Portrait*. New York: Macmillan.

—— (1963) *Moody Without Sankey*. London: Hodder & Stoughton.

Rosell, Garth (ed.) (1999) *Commending the Faith: The Preaching of D. L. Moody*. Peabody, MA: Hendrickson.

Smith, George Adam (1899) *The Life of Henry Drummond*, 2nd ed. London: Hodder & Stoughton.

Smith, Wilbur M. (ed.) (1971) *The Best of D. L. Moody*. Chicago: Moody.

Sweeting, George and Donald (2001) *Lessons from the Life of Moody*. Chicago: Moody Press.

Toone, Mark J. (1998) 'Evangelicalism in Transition: A Comparative Analysis of the Work and Theology of D. L. Moody and His Protégés, Henry Drummond and R. A. Torrey', PhD dissertation, St Andrews University, Scotland.

Torrey, R.A. (1992) *Why God Used D. L. Moody*. Minneapolis: World Wide Publications, reprint.

Ward, Kaari (ed.) (1989) *Great Disasters*. New York: Reader's Digest.

'Where Would Mr Moody Stand?' (1923) *The Christian Century* (12 July): 870–2.

White, John Wesley (1963) 'The Influence of North American Evangelism in Great Britain Between 1830 and 1914 on the Origin and Development of the Ecumenical Movement', PhD dissertation, Mansfield College, Oxford.

NOTES

INTRODUCTION: REMEMBERING MR MOODY

1 Thomas E. Corts (ed.), *Henry Drummond: A Perpetual Benediction* (Edinburgh: T&T Clark, 1999), p. xvi.

CHAPTER 1: DEMYTHOLOGIZING MOODY

1 Charles R. Erdman, *D. L. Moody: His Message for Today* (New York: Revell, 1928), p. 11.
2 Ernest R. Sandeen, *The Roots of Fundamentalism: British and American Millenarianism, 1800–1930* (Chicago: University of Chicago Press, 1970) p. 172; Martin E. Marty in the *Foreword* to James F. Findlay Jr, *Dwight L. Moody: American Evangelist, 1837–1899* (Chicago: University of Chicago Press, 1969), p. 1.
3 For a comprehensive analysis of the theology implicit in Moody's sermons, see my book, *Love Them In: The Life and Theology of D. L. Moody* (Chicago: Moody, 1999).
4 Stan Nussbaum, 'D. L. Moody and the Church: A study of the Ecclesiological Implications of Extra-Ecclesiological Evangelism' (master's thesis, Trinity Evangelical Divinity School, 1973), p. 1 of Abstract and pp. 15–18.
5 Lyman Abbott, 'Snap-Shots of My Contemporaries: Dwight Lyman Moody – Evangelist', *The Outlook* 64 (22 June 1921): 326.
6 William R. Moody, *D. L. Moody* (New York: Macmillan, 1930), p. 212.
7 From a sermon preached in Providence, Rhode Island, on 1 January 1894, according to the 'Elder Son' sermon envelope, Moodyana Collection, Moody Bible Institute. Quoted from an undated, unidentified clipping from a Providence newspaper in that envelope.
8 Charles F. Goss, *Echoes from the Pulpit and the Platform* (Hartford, CT: A. D. Worthington, 1900), pp. 317–19.

9 D. L. Moody, *The London Discourses of Mr D. L. Moody* (London: James Clarke, 1875), pp. 149–51; D. L. Moody, *Wondrous Love: Fifteen Addresses* (London: J. E. Hawkins, c.1875), pp. 261–4; D. L. Moody, *Glad Tidings. Comprising Sermons and Prayer-Meeting Talks Delivered at the New York Hippodrome* (New York: E. B. Treat, 1876), pp. 270–3.

10 D. L. Moody, *New Sermons, Addresses and Prayers* (St Louis, MO: N. D. Thompson, 1877), pp. 137–40; cf. p. 351.

11 'Address Delivered by Mr D. L. Moody, General Conference, Saturday Evening, August 12, 1899', p. 4 of typed manuscript, Moodyana Collection.

12 *Signs of Our Times* (10 March 1875), p. 149.

13 T. J. Shanks (ed.), *A College of Colleges Led by D. L. Moody*, No. 2 (New York: Revell, 1888), pp. 188, 223.

14 'Moody Talks of Faith', *Journal* (New Bedford, MA), undated clipping, but probably 1895, Moodyana Collection.

15 William G. McLoughlin Jr, *Modern Revivalism: Charles Grandison Finney to Billy Graham* (New York: Ronald, 1959), pp. 166–7; also McLoughlin (ed.), *The American Evangelicals, 1800–1900: An Anthology* (New York: Harper & Row, 1968), p. 171.

16 Bernard A. Weisberger, *They Gathered at the River: The Story of the Great Revivalists and Their Impact upon Religion in America* (Boston: Little Brown, 1958), pp. 220–3, 231.

17 William G. McLoughlin Jr, *Billy Sunday Was His Real Name* (Chicago: University of Chicago Press, 1955), p. 158; *Boston Daily Advertiser*, 3 February 1877, p. 4.

18 McLoughlin, *Modern Revivalism*, p. 166.

19 William R. Moody, *The Life of D. L. Moody* (New York: Revell, 1900), p. 281.

20 'The Awakening in Edinburgh', *The Christian*, 29 January 1874, p. 3.

21 *Addresses and Lectures of D. L. Moody, with a Narrative of the Awakening in Liverpool and London* (New York: Anson D. F. Randolph, 1875), pp. 26–35; these pages are a reprint of R. W. Dale's account of the Birmingham meetings that originally appeared in *The Congregationalist*, March 1875.

22 George Adam Smith, *The Life of Henry Drummond* (New York: Hodder & Stoughton, 1898), p. 67.

23 John Hall and George Stuart, *The American Evangelists, D. L. Moody and Ira D. Sankey, in Great Britain and Ireland* (New York: Dodd & Mead, 1875), p. 30.

24 *New Sermons*, p. 587; D. L. Moody, *To All People* (New York: E. B. Treat, 1884), p. 424; D. L. Moody, *Secret Power; or, The Secret of Success in Christian Life and Christian Work* (Chicago: Revell, 1881), p. 110; W. H. Daniels (ed.), *Moody: His Words, Work, and Workers* (New York; Nelson & Phillips, 1877), p. 399.

25 McLoughlin, *Modern Revivalism*, p. 169.

26 J. C. Pollock, *The Keswick Story* (Chicago: Moody, 1964), pp. 66–7.

27 *New Sermons*, pp. 223–4, 263–4, 266, 273, 584–5; 'Ninety-First Psalm Address Delivered by Mr D. L. Moody, Young Women's Conference, Saturday Evening, July 15, 1899', p. 3 of typed manuscript in the Moodyana Collection.

28 *New Sermons*, p. 373; *To All People*, p. 511.

29 *Glad Tidings*, pp. 471–2; *New Sermons*, p. 274.

30 Dwight L. Moody, 'When My Lord Jesus Comes', *The Christian Herald*, 23 February 1910, pp. 168–9; Dwight L. Moody, 'When Jesus Comes Again,' *The Christian Herald*, 21 December 1910, pp. 1208–9.

31 *New Sermons*, pp. 146–64.

32 For documentation of the Unitarian/Universalist attacks on Moody, see *Love Them In*, pp. 119–20.

33 Paul D. Moody, 'Moody Becoming "a Veiled Figure"', *The Christian Century*, 2 August 1923, p. 979.

34 George Adam Smith, 'Dwight L. Moody: A Personal Tribute', *The Outlook*, 20 January 1900, p. 163; Lyman Abbott, 'Snapshots of My Contemporaries: Dwight Lyman Moody – Evangelist', *The Outlook* 64, 22 June 1921, p. 326.

CHAPTER 2: D. L. MOODY:
MORE THAN AN EVANGELIST

1 William R. Moody, *The Life of Dwight L. Moody* (1900), p. 502.
2 Moody to Mrs Jame McKinnon, 12 November 1899, quoted in W. R. Moody, *Life of Moody*, p. 546.
3 Quoted in John McDowell *et al.*, *What D. L. Moody Means to Me* (1937), p. 9.
4 See Lyle W. Dorsett, *A Passion for Souls: The Life of D. L. Moody* (1997). All of my material in the following paragraphs come from this book unless otherwise noted.
5 Paraphrased from 'The Journal of Jane McKinnon', Yale Divinity School Archives and quoted in Dorsett, *A Passion For Souls*.
6 See Lyle W. Dorsett, *Billy Sunday and the Redemption of Urban America* (1991).

CHAPTER 3: THE GREAT TURNING POINT
IN THE LIFE OF D. L. MOODY

1 *Encyclopaedia Britannica*, 1953 ed, s.v. 'Moody, Dwight Lyman.'
2 Letter from Emma Dryer to Charles Blanchard (president of Wheaton College), January 1916, Moody Archives, p. 25.
3 William Sweeting was converted in Bethany Hall. Early in his Christian life my grandfather was enlisted by Tent Hall to go into the Glasgow city centre to assist in open-air meetings. He played in a concertina band that would lead the people back to the Hall for Sunday evening meetings.
4 For more on Moody's life see George Sweeting and Donald Sweeting, *Lessons from the Life of Moody* (Chicago: Moody Press, 2001).
5 John Pollock, *Moody Without Sankey* (London: Hodder & Stoughton, 1963), p. 80.
6 Lyle W. Dorsett, *A Passion for Souls: The Life of D. L. Moody* (Chicago: Moody Press, 1997), pp. 128, 148.
7 Pollock, p. 82.

8 Donald L. Miller, *City of the Century: The Epic of Chicago and the Making of America* (New York: Simon & Schuster, 1996), p. 122.
9 In 1830, Chicago had a population of about 350 people. By 1850, it had risen to about 30,000. In 1860, it reached 112,000.
10 Kaari Ward (ed.), *Great Disasters* (New York: Reader's Digest, 1989), p. 125.
11 Ibid., p. 127.
12 Pollock, p. 85.
13 Ibid.
14 Richard K. Curtis, *They Called Him Mister Moody* (Grand Rapids, MI: Eerdmans, 1962), p. 154. It is worth mentioning that Spafford lost his four little girls in the sinking of a ship, and subsequently wrote the hymn 'It is Well With My Soul'. One wonders if Moody feared a similar loss that night?
15 Ward, p. 128.
16 Donald L. Miller, *City of the Century*, p. 142.
17 Whittle Diary, 2 October 1876.
18 Richard S. Rhodes, *Moody's Latest Sermons* (Chicago: Rhodes & McClure, 1898), pp. 680, 681.
19 James F. Findlay Jr, *Dwight L. Moody: American Evangelist, 1837–1899* (Chicago: University of Chicago Press, 1969). From the Whittle diary quoted on pp. 132, 134.
20 William R. Moody, *The Life of D. L. Moody* (New York: Macmillan, 1930), p. 131.
21 Dorsett, p. 10. From the Foreword by Joseph Stowell.
22 A comment relayed by Anglican Bishop Michael Baughen (Bishop of Chester) to Don Sweeting in a personal conversation.

CHAPTER 4: D. L. MOODY: PAYMENT ON ACCOUNT

1 Theodore Cuyler, quoted in J. C. Pollock, *Moody Without Sankey* (1963), p. 96.
2 Will H. Houghton and Charles T. Cook, *Tell Me About Moody: An International Centenary Tribute to the*

Foremost Evangelist of Modern Times, D. L. Moody, Born February 5, 1837 (1937), p. 23.

3 Ibid., pp. 23–4.

4 *Scotsman*, quoted in Houghton and Cook, *Tell Me About Moody*, p. 29.

5 William R. Moody, *The Life of D. L. Moody* (1900), p. 131.

6 Ibid., pp. 131, 135; Pollock, *Moody Without Sankey*, p. 65, states that Moody wanted to meet George Williams, founder of the YMCA, Müller and Spurgeon. Dorsett concurs, p. 129. Day states that he wanted to meet Williams, Spurgeon and John Darby of the Plymouth Brethren (Richard Ellsworth Day, *Bush Aglow* (1936), p. 121).

7 Arthur T. Pierson, *George Müller of Bristol*, (1899), pp. 248–9.

8 The sources of support and the fund-raising effectiveness of Moody are topics for another paper. In his award-winning biography, *Titan: The Life of John D. Rockefeller Sr*, Ron Chernow, writing about the period around 1883, states that Rockefeller 'gave substantial sums to the revivalist Dwight L. Moody and urged Henry Flagler to follow suit' (Chernow, p. 231).

9 Pollock, *Moody Without Sankey* (London: Hodder & Stoughton, 1963), p. 63.

10 R. Shindler, *From the Usher's Desk to the Tabernacle Pulpit* (1892), p. 208.

11 Pollock, p. 66.

12 Shindler, pp. 208–9.

13 Pollock, pp. 66, 69.

14 George C. Needham, *Recollections of Henry Moorhouse, Evangelist* (1881), p. 109.

15 Ibid., pp. 106–11.

16 W. R. Moody, p. 153.

17 Pollock, pp. 92, 94.

18 W. R. Moody, pp. 152–3; Pollock, pp. 94, 95.

19 W. R. Moody, pp. 153, 154.

20 Ibid., p. 154; Dorsett, pp. 161–2.

21 Arthur Percy Fitt, *Moody Still Lives: Word Pictures of D. L. Moody* (1936), p. 28.

22 Ibid., pp. 54, 55.

23 Ibid., pp. 55–6; Pollock, p. 94.
24 Fitt, p. 56; Pollock, p. 96.
25 Pollock, pp. 95–6.
26 Ibid., p. 96.
27 W. R. Moody, p. 154.
28 Pollock, p. 96.
29 Fitt, p. 57; Pollock, p. 97.
30 Pollock, p. 98.
31 M. Jennie Street, *F. B. Meyer: His Life and Work* (1902), pp. 40–3; A. Chester Mann, *F. B. Meyer: Preacher, Teacher, Man of God* (1929), pp. 115–18.
32 W. R. Moody, p. 161.
33 Ira D. Sankey, *Sankey's Story of the Gospel Hymns* (1906), p. 23.
34 W. R. Moody, p. 170.
35 J. Wilbur Chapman, *Life and Work of Dwight Lyman Moody* (1900), p. 31.
36 W. Robertson Nicoll, *Princes of the Church* (1921), p. 97.
37 W. R. Moody, p. 238.
38 Ibid., p. 297.
39 Nicoll, *Princes of the Church*, pp. 56–7.
40 Ibid., p. 57.
41 The Rev. Alex Rattray, in Professor Fergus Ferguson, *The Life of the Rev. Dr Andrew A. Bonar*, n.d., pp. 192–3.
42 Pollock, p. 113; the other was Lord Cairns; W. R. Moody, *Life of Dwight L. Moody*, p. 257.
43 Pollock, p. 252.
44 Ibid., pp. 305–6.
45 Fitt, p. 66.
46 Quoted in Pollock, p. 210; Fitt, *Moody Still Lives*, p. 66.
47 Stanley High, *Billy Graham: The Personal Story of the Man, His Message and His Mission* (1956), p. 171.
48 Now known as the University of Westminster, a plaque noting that London Polytechnic was founded by Quintin Hogg is on the main building just north of Oxford Circus, not far from All Souls, Langham Place. On its website in 2003, the University of Westminster noted that Quintin Hogg acquired the institution at 309 Regent Street in 1881 after a fire and financial difficulties. The website noted that Hogg had been working to benefit the poor and working

people of London for about twenty years and running his Young Men's Christian Institution in Covent Garden since 1871.

49 Pollock, p. 210.
50 Ibid., p. 215.
51 Ibid., p. 215.
52 Ibid., p. 219.
53 Ibid., p. 254.
54 Ibid., p. 128.
55 W. R. Moody, p. 394.
56 Ibid., p. 395.
57 Ibid., pp. 398–9.
58 Ibid., pp. 400–7.
59 Quoted in *Souvenir Programme of Moody National Centenary Celebration*, Royal Albert Hall, 5 February 1937.
60 A copy of the programme for the event is in the collection of the British Library, London.
61 'Our Monthly Survey: The Moody and Sankey Revival', *The Sunday Magazine*, IV new series (1875), p. 857.
62 The Reverend Newman Hall was a leading evangelical minister of that day. Elias Nason, *The American Evangelists* (1877), p. 121.
63 Pollock, pp. 209–10.
64 'Our Monthly Survey: Two Noble Lords on Messrs Moody and Sankey', *The Sunday Magazine*, IV new series (1875), p. 642.
65 Pollock, p. 143.
66 James F. Findlay, Jr., *Dwight L. Moody: American Evangelist 1837–1899* (1969), pp. 179–80; Pollock, pp. 147ff.
67 Mrs Robert Peddie (ed.), *A Conservative Narrative of the Remarkable Awakening in Edinburgh* (1874), p. 8.
68 Mrs Peddie, *A Conservative Narrative*, p. 39.
69 Pollock, p. 144.
70 Chapman, p. 93.
71 Burnham Carter, *So Much to Learn: The History of Northfield Mount Hermon School in Commemoration of the 100th Anniversary 1980* (1976), p. 49.
72 Ibid.
73 G. D. Pike, *The Jubilee Singers and Their Campaign for Twenty Thousand Dollars* (1873), p. 77.

74 *The Great Revival: Being An Account of the Evangelistic Labours, in the United Kingdom of Messrs Moody and Sankey*, p. 7.

75 Mrs Peddie, *A Conservative Narrative*, p. 45. 'It is a coincidence worthy of note that more than half the melodies in this collection are in the same scale as that in which Scottish music is written; that is, with the fourth and the seventh tones omitted.' Theo. F. Seward in Pike, *The Jubilee Singers*, p. 164.

76 Mrs Peddie, pp. 45–6.

77 Joe M. Richardson, *A History of Fisk University* (1980), p. 36.

78 Ibid., p. 36.

79 For a more detailed discussion of Moody and race, see Findlay, pp. 278–81.

80 Kyle W. Dorsett, *A Passion for Souls: The Life of D. L. Moody* (1997), pp. 165–9.

81 Mark James Toone, 'Evangelicalism in Transition: A Comparative Analysis of the Work and Theology of D. L. Moody and His Protégés, Henry Drummond and R. A. Torrey', PhD dissertation, 1988, University of St Andrews, p. 94.

82 Dorsett, *A Passion for Souls*, p. 168.

83 Ibid., pp. 214–15.

84 Lord and Lady Aberdeen, *We Twa: The Reminiscences of Lord and Lady Aberdeen* (1925), I, p. 302.

85 Ibid., I, pp. 302.

86 Peddie, p. 48.

87 W. R. Moody, p. 199.

88 Janet Mabie, *The Years Beyond: The Story of Northfield, D. L. Moody, and The Schools* (1960), p. 166.

89 Dorsett, pp. 252–4.

90 Ibid., p. 57.

91 Ibid., pp. 62–3, 69–70; Carter, *So Much to Learn*, p. 71.

92 Mrs Peddie, p. 37.

93 *The Great Revival: Being An Account of the Evangelistic Labours in the United Kingdom of Messrs Moody & Sankey Compiled by the Editors of* Church and Home (1875), p. 7.

94 'Topics of the Time: Revivals and Evangelists', *Scribner's Monthly* 11 (April 1876): 887.

95 J. H. Crespi, 'Moody and Sankey', *The Southern Review* 19 (January 1876): 194.
96 Ibid., p. 195.
97 John D. Hall, *The American Evangelists* (1875), p. 6.
98 W. R. Moody, p. 227.
99 Ibid., p. 215.
100 Hall, p. 30.
101 Mrs Peddie, p. 65.
102 Ibid., p. 49.
103 *The Great Revival . . . Compiled by the Editor of* Church and Home, p. 8; E. J. Goodspeed, *A Full History of the Wonderful Career of Moody and Sankey in Great Britain and America* (1876), p. 148.
104 Goodspeed, *A Full History*, p. 148.
105 *The Great Revival . . . Compiled by the Editors of* Church and Home, p. 8.
106 J. C. Pollock, *The Cambridge Seven: A Call to Christian Service* (1955).
107 M. Jennie Street, *F. B. Meyer: His Life and Work* (1902), pp. 40–3.
108 George Adam Smith, *The Life of Henry Drummond*, pp. 54–100.
109 Dorsett, pp. 220–1.
110 *The Quiver*, IX (1884): 684.
111 Ibid.
112 T. H. Darlow, *William Robertson Nicoll: Life and Letters*, p. 28.

CHAPTER 5: MOODY AS A
TRANSATLANTIC EVANGELICAL

1 Stanley N. Gundry, *Love Them In: The Life and Theology of D. L. Moody* (Chicago: Moody Press, 1999), pp. 131–2. I am grateful to Stan Gundry for sending me a copy of the new edition of his study of Moody's theology.
2 *D. L. Moody at Home* (London: Morgan & Scott, n.d.), p. 12.
3 W. H. Daniels, *D. L. Moody and His Work* (London: Hodder & Stoughton, 1875), p. 426.

4 Gundry, p. 170.
5 R. Shindler, *From the Usher's Desk to the Tabernacle Pulpit: The Life and Labours of Pastor C. H. Spurgeon* (London: Passmore & Alabaster, 1892), p. 208.
6 James F. Findlay Jr, *Dwight L. Moody: American Evangelist, 1837–1899* (Chicago: University of Chicago Press, 1969), p. 35. Basic biographical information is taken from this standard life of Moody.
7 *D. L. Moody at Home*, p. 11.
8 Henry Drummond, *Dwight L. Moody: Impressions and Facts* (New York: McClure, Philips, 1900), p. 40.
9 George E. Morgan, '*A Veteran in Revival*': *R. C. Morgan: His Life and Times* (London: Morgan & Scott, 1909), p. 209.
10 Kathryn T. Long, *The Revival of 1857–58* (New York: Oxford University Press, 1998), p. 127.
11 Findlay, p. 164.
12 John Macpherson, *Henry Moorhouse: The English Evangelist* (London: Morgan & Scott, n.d.), p. 51.
13 Ibid., pp. 66, 90.
14 Ian Hamilton, *The Erosion of Calvinist Orthodoxy* (Edinburgh: Rutherford House Books, 1990), chap. 3.
15 *D. L. Moody at Home*, pp. 14, 17.
16 Findlay, p. 313, n.18.
17 Drummond, p. 56.
18 Gundry, p. 35.
19 Drummond, p. 87.
20 Findlay, p. 364, n. 51.
21 Drummond, pp. 91–3.
22 Ibid., p. 112.
23 J. C. Pollock, *Moody without Sankey: A New Biographical Portrait* (London: Hodder & Stoughton, 1963), pp. 67–8.
24 A. W. W. Dale, *The Life of R. W. Dale of Birmingham* (London: Hodder & Stoughton, 1898), p. 334.
25 Gundry, p. 215.
26 Ibid., p. 153.
27 *D. L. Moody at Home*, p. 113.
28 Long, p. 91.
29 Horatius Bonar in *The Christian*, 8 January 1874, p. 7.
30 Moody in *The Christian*, 22 January 1874, p. 7.

31 Peter Bailey, *Leisure and Class in Victorian England: Rational Recreation and the Contest for Control, 1830–1885* (London: Routledge & Kegan Paul, 1978), chap. 7.
32 Dale, p. 319.
33 Gundry, p. 141.
34 D. L. Moody, *Notes from My Bible* (London: Morgan & Scott, n.d.), p. 121.
35 Gundry, p. 141.
36 Ibid., p. 45, chap. 4, pp. 97–102, 43.
37 *D. L. Moody at Home*, p. 31.
38 Moody, p. 30.
39 Findlay, pp. 406–7.
40 Moody, p. 43.
41 Findlay, p. 132.
42 T. H. Bainbridge, *Reminiscences*, ed. Gerald France (London: C.H. Kelly, 1913), pp. 55, 67.
43 Findlay, p. 407, n. 37.
44 *The Christian*, 19 August 1875, p. 9.
45 *The Christian*, 22 January 1874, p. 5; 7 May 1874, p. 7.
46 Pollock, p. 211.
47 *D. L. Moody at Home*, p. 21.
48 Clyde Binfield, *George Williams and the YMCA: A Study in Victorian Social Attitudes* (London: Heinemann, 1973), p. 225.
49 Pollock, p. 145.
50 Ibid., p. 142.
51 John Kent, *Holding the Fort: Studies in Victorian Revivalism* (London: Epworth Press, 1978), chaps 4–6, 9.
52 Findlay, pp. 71, 73, 326–7.
53 Gundry, p. 163, n. 8.
54 John Coffey, 'Democracy and Popular Religion: Moody and Sankey's Mission to Britain, 1873–1875', in Eugenio F. Biagini (ed.), *Citizenship and Community: Liberals, Radicals and Collective Identities in the British Isles, 1865–1931* (Cambridge: Cambridge University Press, 1996), p. 97.
55 Pollock, pp. 147–9.
56 Coffey, p. 107.
57 I. G. C. Hutchinson, *A Political History of Scotland, 1832–1924: Parties, Elections and Issues* (Edinburgh: John Donald, 1986), pp. 136–8.

58 *The Christian*, 22 January 1874, p. 6.
59 Morgan, p. 52.
60 Long, p. 125.
61 Gundry, p. 97.
62 Findlay, p. 361.
63 Gundry, p. 155.
64 *D. L. Moody at Home*, p. 112.
65 Ibid., p. 183.
66 Drummond, p. 70.
67 Gundry, p. 126.
68 Findlay, pp. 397, n. 16.
69 F. V. Waddleton, 'The Bible Training Institute, Glasgow' (unpublished manuscript [1979]), pp. 11–12.
70 Gundry, p. 174.
71 George Adam Smith in Drummond, pp. 25, 28.
72 Drummond, p. 40.
73 Smith in ibid., p. 15.
74 *D. L. Moody at Home*, p. 108.
75 Marjorie Bonar (ed.), *Andrew A. Bonar. DD: Life and Letters* (London: Hodder & Stoughton, 1893), p. 245.
76 Findlay, p. 369.
77 Smith in Drummond, p. 4.
78 Morgan, pp. 184–5.
79 Malcolm Prentis, 'City of God, City of Man: Images of the Slum, 1897–1911', in Lynette Finch and Chris McConville (eds), *Gritty Cities: Images of the Urban* (Annandale, NSW: Pluto Press, 1999), pp. 104–7.

CHAPTER 6: D. L. MOODY AND REVIVALISM

1 Iain Murray, *Revival and Revivalism, The Making and Marring of American Evangelicalism* (Edinburgh: The Banner of Truth Trust), p. xix.
2 Ibid.
3 David Breed, 'The New England in Evangelism', *Princeton Theological Review*: (Philadelphia, 1903), p. 229.
4 James F. Findlay Jr, *Dwight L. Moody: American Evangelist 1837–1899* (Chicago and London: University of Chicago Press, 1969), pp. 203–4.

5 Findlay, p. 210.
6 Murray, p. 412.
7 *Reminiscences of Revival of '59* (Aberdeen, 1910), pp. 15–16.

CHAPTER 7: D. L. MOODY AND CHURCH MUSIC

1 I refer here, with respect and love, to Billy Graham, with whom I served as a full-time crusade musician from 1960 to 1967.
2 John Pollock, *Moody without Sankey* (reprint, Christian Focus Publications Ltd, Geanies House, Fearn, Ross-shire, IV20 1TW, Scotland, 1963), p. 87.
3 Ibid.
4 See note no. 2.
5 Pollock, p. 87.
6 Pollock, p. 88.
7 Pollock, p. 91.
8 Ira D. Sankey, *My Life and the Story of the Gospel Hymns* (New York: Harper & Brothers, 1907), p. 60.
9 Ibid., p. 268.
10 James F. Findlay Jr, *Dwight L. Moody, American Evangelist* (Chicago: University of Chicago Press, 1969), p. 214.
11 Pollock, p. 145.
12 Don Randel (ed.), *The New Harvard Dictionary of Music* (Cambridge, MA: Harvard University Press, 1986), p. 344.
13 Findlay, p. 369.
14 Gene A. Getz, *MBI: The Story of Moody Bible Institute* (Chicago: Moody Press, 1969), p. 63.
15 Wm J. Reynolds, *The Cross and the Lyre* (Fort Worth, Tex.: Southwestern Baptist Theological Seminary, 1994), p. 4.

CHAPTER 8: POWER – 'IN' AND 'UPON':
A MOODY SERMON

1 C. S. Lewis, *Surprised by Joy* (London: Fontana, 1959), p. 182.
2 Lewis, p. 182.

3 Matthew Parris, *I Couldn't Possible Comment* (London: Robson Books, 1997), p. 53.

4 Lyle Dorsett, *A Passion for Souls: The Life of D. L. Moody* (Chicago: Moody Press, 1997), pp. 128, 244–5.

5 Dorsett, p. 164.

6 John Pollock, *Moody Without Sankey* (London: Hodder & Stoughton, 1996 edn), p. 99.

7 Dorsett, p. 21.

8 The phrase 'duchesses and dockers' is the title (in reverse) of Pollock's chapter 18, *op. cit.*

9 See Pollock, pp. 65–74.

10 Dorsett, p. 156.

11 Dorsett, pp. 161–2.

12 James F. Findlay Jr, *Dwight L. Moody: American Evangelist, 1837–1899* (Chicago and London: University of Chicago Press, 1969), p. 237.

13 Findlay, pp. 237–9.

14 D. L. Moody, 'Power – "in" and "upon" ', *Conversion, Service and Glory* (London: Morgan & Scott, n.d.), p. 183.

15 Throughout this chapter the King James Version has been used since Moody himself did so.

16 Moody, pp. 184ff.

17 Ibid., p. 185.

18 Ibid., p. 173.

19 This should not be taken as justification for refusing to change and adapt to contemporary culture. It is to say that the basic answer to the church's problems is not to be found there.

20 This paragraph is dependent on Moody, pp. 178–82 and 186.

21 Moody, p. 180.

22 David Bebbington, *Evangelicalism in Modern Britain* (London: Unwin Hyman, 1989), pp. 10–12.

23 Mark Noll, *The Scandal of the Evangelical Mind* (Grand Rapids, MI: Eerdmans, 1994), p. 243.

24 Moody, p. 183.

25 Ibid., p. 187.

26 Ibid., p. 189.

27 1 Cor. 1:18–2:5.

28 2 Cor. 4:6.
29 Moody, p. 182.
30 Ibid., p. 189.
31 Ibid., p. 185.
32 Ibid., p. 191.

INDEX